Number 4
A Chinese Prison Story
Part 1
Pik Uk
Stewart Burton

Foreword

By Chris Forse, History Teacher 1974-2006, Head of History 1983-1988,Vice Principal 1988-2006, Island School

It was the beginning of the 1989-90 school year at Island School in Hong Kong. We were loosely defined as an 'international school' but in reality, still a 'British school', a colonial creation providing the British expatriate community with what they might expect at home: O Levels (now GCSEs) and A Levels. As it happened, we were by then attracting a more global intake along with some offspring of well-heeled local Chinese parents. I was Head of Sixth Form.

Early that school year I received an admissions application from a Mr and Mrs Cuthbertson for their sixteen-year-old son Stewart to join a Sixth Form groaning under the weight of numbers (approaching 300) and shortage of teaching space. But, hey, what was one more applicant? Stewart was British, a product of the Scottish school system; his parents were entitled to apply. An interview was set up.

Stewart, as it turned out, was no ordinary applicant. Whereas most, if not all, our applicants came from other schools, whether in the UK, Hong Kong or globally, Stewart was not at school at all. He was in the Royal Navy having left school that summer. Such an application would, as a matter of course, raise suspicions that there were opaque reasons for his parents wanting him to join them in Hong Kong: was he an expellee, had had already been cashiered by the Navy, had he been involved in crime or drugs?

The boy who turned up for that interview with his

parents was not like 'our students': he was pale and wan, undernourished, possibly. He was polite but uncommunicative. I tried to draw him out on why he was leaving the navy to return to school and received what looked like rehearsed answers about wanting 'a second go'.

My head was saying 'don't touch this'. How would this young man ever fit into a school community of 'nowhere citizens', bright, confident and worldly (though not necessarily worldly-wise) students. But my heart (and our admissions policy) told me otherwise: why should I not give this young man a chance to enjoy the fruits of a Hong Kong education.

We were not a selective school though our happy medium lay at the upper end of the educational spectrum as measured by exam results and university entrance. We were, to our shame, not geared up to provide support for anything other than mild special needs demands, and none at all in the Sixth Form. Words like 'autism' and acronyms like 'ADD and ADHD' had barely registered in our consciousness; they had barely registered in anyone's consciousness at that time, least of all in colonial Hong Kong.

We liked to think we were a 'liberal' school: open and diverse, child-centred and optimistic. And though we were naturally inclined to risk taking, I accepted that Stewart's' admission was indeed a 'risk'. I held my breath. As it turned out by Christmas, I could reflect that I could not have been more wrong in my doubts. Stewart not only took to his new compatriots with relish; they took to him.

And then, come the Spring, he was gone. Expelled. He had, apparently, been accused of trying to sell drugs to younger students. I felt a mix of embarrassment (how could I have been so naïve?) and of an empty disappointment. I took the narrative of his dismissal at face value and tried to ignore the unspoken, 'I told you so' innuendos of others.

Then, come the next school year, I heard that Stewart had been arrested. The story was that he had held up a taxi driver at knifepoint for money to feed a drug habit. I was now fully signed up to the 'wrong 'un' narrative.

It was some weeks later that I received a call from an ex-student, now barrister, Luke McGuinniety, Stewart's court-appointed attorney. He asked if I would be willing to attend Stewart's committal hearing. He had been abandoned by his parents; they had returned to Scotland. He had no one. How utterly tragic. It never occurred to me to do anything other than attend in those circumstances.

We exchanged a few words: "hello, Mr Forse'" . He looked out of it: confused, abandoned and frightened. And the judge sent him down: three years imprisonment in one (or more) of Hong Kong's notorious jails.

Surely it would not actually come to this. I assumed, wrongly, that he would be deported and allowed to serve his sentence in a British jail with people who at least spoke his language. Had I known that he would be incarcerated in Pik Uk prison with hardened criminals, many of whom inhabited the underworld of triad loyalties and honour codes, I would have arranged to visit him.

It was all of twenty-seven years (a Mandela life sentence) later, when we met again, that I discovered the true story of Stewart's imprisonment, now relayed in this gut-wrenching book, 'Number 4'.

Stewart, now Burton (after his maternal grandmother), got in touch with me in the late noughties, to thank me for having been there on his sentencing. He updated me on his life story. He was now a counsellor for young offenders in Glasgow, happily married with a bonny 'wee' boy. I found the news of his rehabilitation inspiring. But I had not heard half (even a quarter) of the reality of Stewart's experiences as an inmate and later deportee, nor of his remarkable rehabilitation in subsequent years.

As the school's fiftieth anniversary approached in 2017, Stewart got back in touch. He was considering attending the celebration, even though he understood that a new name and identity might not shield him from a second deportation, before he even set foot beyond the immigration counters at Hong Kong's Chek Lap Kok airport. 'Go for it' was my advice.

And then we met, fortuitously as it turned out, out on the street beyond the school boundaries as Stewart was making his way up to school as a volunteer in setting out playgrounds and hall for the great Block Party that was to follow that evening.

It was an emotional reunion. I got the 'edited highlights' of his story. "You must write a book". I said. "I plan to'" he responded.

Here it is!

Stewart's story is made all the more remarkable and inspirational given the nature of that rehabilitation: from counsellor for young offenders, to a master's degree in autism within the prison system, to a career in education, including the headship of a school in India, and to a growing international reputation as an authority on autism. It is a cliché to say that everyone, no matter what ills befall them, whether self-inflicted or socially determined, is worth a second chance. Stewart's story is a full-blooded, raw, and shocking validation of that age's old narrative.

And when Stewart sent me a draft of his memories in

'Number 4', I reflected on what I could learn, or should have learned, had I known, from his experiences, about the role of educators in facilitating second chances, on never giving up on anyone.

That first draft was gut-wrenching. I questioned whether it should be published raw or refined. The rawness added to the story's power, even if it lacked a comma or two. Now, thanks to support from a group of his f\ormer students, his story, appropriately refined, will air, both in print, here, and eventually in digital documentary form.

I am proud to give some brief thoughts in this Foreword on what is a salutary story of faith and forgiveness, and of the power that lies in us all to overcome even the most traumatic experiences, to discover the goodness that lies in us all.

Chris Forse

Introduction

What a journey. Without Martin, Matt and Zara, a journey that was fated never to end, an indeterminate prison sentence, life without parole etc.

They weren't the only ones I pestered over the years. There are many poor souls to add to the list.

Huge thanks to Chris Forse and Sean Ellis who were the ones to suggest I do this in the first place back in 2017 at the Island School 50th anniversary reunion. Also, to Sean for interviewing me for his documentary on the school.

Anna, who was my first agent. She, with a pile of crap, tried her best to move the project forward and gave me huge support at the beginning.

When it all looked like it wasn't going anywhere, Alan Roth popped up and only with his continuous belief in my writing did I continue. It was Alan that persuaded me to rewrite the book and to put it into two parts, just in case any TV producers are paying attention and want to make it into two series!

In 2019, at a philosophy lecture discussing camouflaging within the female autistic community, a young German lassie named Kat introduced herself to me, perhaps to her own regret.

Kat, you've been here for me the last five years through thick and thin. All the highs and lows that go together with writing something like this. You were also there for me through my argument with cancer, the loss of wee Juno, my heart attack and my divorce. If I've missed anything, I'm sure you will remind me!

All our lives are affected by our connection to our families. My story is no different. Often, these traumas are passed on to our own kids but while I was working very hard to recover from my issues, I have also tried my hardest to stop that wheel from turning.

Dexter and Weston are my two boys who I dedicate this book to, along with their wee half-sister Juno.

We got there boys.

第一章

I am sure it was an old school bus that we were in. I was sitting right at the back, handcuffed to my neighbour. It was freezing cold outside, and black. All the windows were open, but nobody tried to close them. Nobody was moving, talking, doing anything. We all knew better. Although I did not know the language, the threat of violence from the guards was obvious. I did not know where we were going, I was terrified.

When the bus finally stopped it had pulled up at a set of large gates that looked two or even three stories high.

Prison gates. The huge walls running away from their sides could not be seen but were imagined. I did not know what I was expecting; I did not know anything. I was so filled with dread that, for a moment, the pain I was feeling right through my body was a dull ache in the background.

The gates opened slowly like they were going to consume us, and they did. The bus drove through them into a vast room where it stopped. My whole body tensed with anticipation, and some more guards came onto the bus. They walked up the aisle of the bus like the devil's own air stewards, counting their unfortunate passengers who were heading to hell. The bus then drove through into the prison compound.

When the doors opened, a guard stood up and shouted something and all the other prisoners stood up to get off the bus. I followed. After we had disembarked, they made us stand in a line and then a guard came and removed our handcuffs. We had been chained two by two and, when we were separated, we were made to stand in single file. I could not tell if I was shaking from physical pain or psychological terror. I was shivering from head to toe. I looked up and tried to take in my surroundings.

It was dark and the whole place was covered in a thick fog. Orange lights were shining through it which gave off enough light for me to make out high fences surrounding me on two sides. There were buildings in front of me that I could just make out through the darkness and fog. I also noticed grey fences leading off in different directions. As my eyes started to adjust, I could see the source of the main lights. In turrets on top of the walls, there were spotlights staffed by armed guards. I could see their guns, the gun barrels shining in the dark, moist from the rain.

We were lined up facing a door. All I could make out was an orange glow coming from it. There were guards shouting orders at each of the prisoners and they walked through the glow, one by one, into the room beyond. One guard came out; he was wearing a white coat and an officer's cap. He was coming down the line shouting at everyone he passed. He pushed a few of the others in front of me and I could see their bodies were rigid with fear as he approached them. Some he seemed to recognise, he would talk to them quietly like an uncle, and then, without warning, he would punch them in the stomach. They would try not to show pain, they would stand as still as they could. It was as if they showed any reaction, he would do it again. A couple of times he did.

He finally got to me. He stood there looking at my sorry state, shivering in the freezing cold. He came right up close to me, so close I could smell him. I was scared, very scared. He whispered to me in a very heavy Chinese accent in English.

'I can help you.'

For a fleeting moment, I believed him. I wanted to believe him.

'Come with me'.

I followed him past the others to the bright orange glow of the door. Now I could see inside. It was like a doctor's waiting room. Three of the guys who were in the queue in front of me were already in the room. They were naked. There were three big men in white coats in different corners, each one with a naked guy. I slowly started taking it in. I was terrified. I was pushed to the left. The guard laughed and shouted at me.

'See I told you I could help you, now strip'.

I stood there; he came right up to me with his baton and rammed it into my stomach. I nearly crumpled to the floor. 'Strip' and then he started ripping at my clothes.

'Do you not understand me, Gwai Gi [foreign devil boy]?'

I just had to do it; I had no choice. I took my clothes off. I stopped at my underwear and he shouted, 'Everything'. I took my underwear off. I was standing there naked and freezing, I felt ashamed and scared. My shivering was now a mixture of cold and fear.

A guy in a white coat then grabbed me. He had surgical gloves on and he grabbed my head. He pulled at my hair and my ears. He pulled my mouth open and looked inside; he grabbed my arms and raised them over my head. He told me to spread my legs and pull up my testicles. He grabbed my penis and told me to pull my foreskin back. I could hear other guys going through other treatments, but I dared not look around. I was then pushed over to another white coat. There was a chair next to him; he shouted something in Chinese I could not understand. I stood there. He punched me in the stomach. He shouted again, this time pointing at the chair which had its back to me, I went to turn the chair around, and I was punched again. He shouted in English.

'Bend over'.

I was now truly terrified. If I thought that I had already been assaulted, it was about to get worse. I was pushed over the chair, another guard grabbed my arms and pulled me forward, my legs were kicked apart and I was held there. The guard came round and looked me in the eyes. He also had surgical gloves on. He put his hand into a large pot and pulled out a handful of grease. He slowly rubbed the grease into his hands, smiled and walked round to my back. I started struggling but the guards just pushed me down. I felt his hands cold against my buttocks. He spread them apart and slowly pushed a finger up my back passage. It was agony but I could not cry, I dared not. He pushed deeper and deeper and started feeling about, laughing as he did it. Then he whipped his finger out, I was let go of and then pushed to another table. I felt that I had just been raped. I had been degraded to my very core.

Nothing could have been worse. I wanted to die right there; it would have been a relief. Little did I know that this would happen to me many times over the next few years. Every time I left the prison and came back from anywhere the same thing would happen. This was true hell, the day before my 18th birthday.

At the next table, I barely heard what the guard said. I was in shock. He was asking if I had any health issues. I just kept saying, 'No, no'. I was then pushed into another room. It was a small dark room that stank of damp, sick bodies and misery. There were about five rows of wooden benches at which some prisoners were sitting. They all had clothes on. I looked down. In front of me, there was a large wicker box full of clothes. I was told to get dressed. I found some trousers and a shirt. They stank and were covered in stains; they were a light blue colour and made of a material that scraped my skin. No underwear.

Next to it was a pile of plastic sandals. I found a pair that fit and was then pushed onto one of the benches. My body ached. I did not know it, but I was going through withdrawal symptoms. It was like a serious bout of flu. Every bone in my body ached. My skin felt so thin that when I sat down, it felt like I was sitting on bare bones.

I was then told to come forward, I was pushed against a wall and had my photo taken. Then I was pushed back to my bench. Some of the guys were having their hair shaved off. We sat there until everyone had been processed. There was no talking. Nobody even acknowledged each other. There was so much depression in the room you could feel it, smell it. After what seemed like an hour, a guard came in and started shouting at us to come forward one by one.

'Gwai Gi hai sun [foreign devil boy get up]', he shouted whilst looking at me.

I copied what the other guys did, stood up and went forward. He gave me a small card which had my photo on it, my name, the letters 'YR' and the number 27343.

'Yee chat sam say sam, cho die [27343 sit down]', he shouted at me.

I looked at him, blankly.

'Yee chat sam say sam cho die', he shouted louder and shoved me back to emphasise the point. I sat down.

We were then told to get up and move outside. We were made to stand side by side. There were new guards now. Everything that they said was in Chinese. I could not understand anything. The guards came to each one of us when they were shouting the orders, right up into our faces, shouting, spit flying out of their mouths onto us.

We were marched two by two into the fog. Gate after gate opened and closed behind us. We walked through long, open corridors of grey metal fences. In the distance, large buildings started to come into sight. We moved towards one of them. It was four stories high, a large, long concrete building. It was difficult to make anything else out in the dark with big powerful lights shining on us from overhead.

We were moved inside. More and more concrete everywhere. The guards continued to shout at us. We were led up some cold concrete stairs up to the second floor. Two prisoners were squatting next to two large blue buckets. We went up to them, one by one, and were given a yellow mug of brown liquid and a plate of rice with a fish head on it. I was instantly repulsed by the sight of it but I took the mug and plate offered. I had clearly already started learning to obey orders as I knew there was no way that I could possibly eat it.

Pushed around a corner to a gate that opened to a long corridor. Dirty slatted windows on one side, a line of bars on the other. The floor and ceiling were concrete. A dull light hung every few metres along the ceiling. I was moved down the corridor. After a few metres, I was stopped and pushed through a gap in the bars. The bars were slammed closed behind me.

A cell. I could not see at first, it was so dark although there was a light on the ceiling. The dark was heavy and thick. I could stretch my arms out and touch each side of the cell. The walls were cold concrete. On one side was a wooden plank on a metal frame, a bed. I walked further in. A metal sink was encased in concrete on the back wall. Next to that, behind a low concrete wall, a hole in the ground, the toilet.

As if that wasn't all bad enough, the noise brought a further dose of reality, the metal clanking of cell doors being slammed and shouting from the guards. Then the lights went out. Whatever small amount of light we'd had previously was virtually gone, just a very low glow from the lights outside my cell remained.

It was then that I finally broke down. I wanted out. I found a button on the wall which I started pressing furiously. A guard came over and I pleaded with him to let me out, I wanted to go home, I should not be there. I was having a panic attack, crying uncontrollably and shaking. He shouted at me and left. As soon as he left me, the noise started. It was as if the whole building erupted into life. There was banging and a thousand Chinese voices all shouting at once. The noise was deafening. Then the screaming started, it was me.

Chapter One

The late 70s and early 80s marked Glasgow's decay after former industrial greatness. Rough and tough, the city centre was a dangerous place full of alcoholics, drug addicts, poverty and crime. I did not live there, however, I was in the suburbs, where footballers lived and where buses travelled infrequently.

Newton Mearns was seen as the place to raise a family back then, with its big houses and quiet streets. No outside toilets there. No pubs either, not the thing in this posh area where every daddy worked and every mummy was the perfect housewife.

We had fields on which to play football, woods to build dens and streams to catch fish. We were safe from the dangers of the outside world. That is what our parents wanted and worked hard to maintain for us, somewhere they did not have to worry about their children. Schools that would take care of all our needs. Idyllic complacency.

My mum always said that she couldn't get me a birthday cake or card for my 'special' day because it was just after new year and all the shops were shut. I do remember getting presents sometimes, but parties didn't happen because I had been born at the wrong time of the year. Nothing could be done about it and because of the time of year I was born, I was also always the youngest in my class at school.

There isn't much that I can remember before going to school. One thing I do know is that I could read before I started school. It was my solace and it still is. I had read the Encyclopaedia Britannica Children's Edition by the time I was 5. It was somewhere I could escape to. I was an easy child so I was left to my own devices most of the time. My father was in the merchant navy and was away from home for many months at a time, so it was left to my mum to raise us.

I don't remember everything about my first day at school but I do remember one specific event. We were all sitting at our desks and I looked over to see this boy crying. I remember being confused by it and found myself getting up and going over to sit next to him. I didn't know the boy and didn't know why he was crying. I just stared at him, I think, and asked him what the matter was.

I was then shouted at by the teacher and told to go back to my seat. I think I must have answered the teacher back and so was shouted at and told to go and stand in the corner. That corner and I got to know each other very well over the next few weeks up until I was promoted to being sent to the office instead.

That contact with the crying boy had been my first attempt to connect with someone of the same age and it was met with punishment. For someone who had huge social difficulties, this one incident on the very first day of school taught me that showing concern for others was frowned upon.

The next event I can remember drawing faces all over my school jotter one day. Every page was full of round heads, two eyes and a mouth. The only thing different in each picture were the mouths. A couple of friends sitting near me laughed so I kept on drawing and drawing until the entire jotter was full of these emotions.

This was my first attempt at understanding the human condition. I have been trying to comprehend it ever since. I came to learn much later that I have prosopagnosia, face blindness, making it difficult for me to recognise people. This, together with my inability to read emotions on people's faces likely generated the artwork in my jotter. The artwork was one of my many 'office' offences.

Any time I was sent to the office, a huge surge of panic would overwhelm my body, but it didn't stop my bad behaviour. Individuals with autism spectrum disorder generally find it difficult to break the rules as we enjoy rigid and fixed instructions. This helps us to feel calm in a world of constant change. However, I now realise that I persisted with the poor behaviour because it meant that I would get the attention that I did not receive at home. After school, I would always just go home and head straight into my room to read.

Letters from the school sent home with me became a regular occurrence, detailing the misdemeanours that I had committed that day. A particularly memorable one was flooding the bathroom by stuffing toilet paper into the plug hole and leaving the tap running. I also used to wet toilet paper and throw it onto the ceiling.

I was very easily led. I thought that doing whatever my friends suggested was how friendships worked. But I was always the one that got caught. I struggled with the social side of school. I didn't play with the other kids much; I didn't know how to or how to make good friends. I tried to copy others' behaviours so that I would be liked, but it never seemed to work for me. I was only 5 years old at this point but I was already struggling badly.

Previously, I thought this was because I didn't have a father figure at home who played with me and who taught me life's rules. Whenever my father was home, he mainly did jobs around the house and then sat and watched television whilst drinking a bottle of Bacardi whilst my mum drank whisky.

But he was away for eight to ten months of the year and then we lived by my mum's rules. While he was away, we ate dinner in front of the television and she gave us whatever we wanted to eat. Never a vegetable or a piece of fruit in sight.

However, when my father was home, all the rules changed. He would make us sit down with him one by one and go through what we wanted for breakfast, lunch and dinner for the two or three weeks that he was home. It would last for hours. I can still remember it now.

'What meat do you want in two weeks on Thursday and what vegetable do you want with it?'

He would write everything down and stick it to the inside of the kitchen cupboard. And when it came to two weeks on Thursday and you were served the chicken and peas that you had ordered, you had to eat them. I had to stay at the table until I had finished everything on the plate.

My younger brother got away with it and my older brother ate everything anyway. But I was left at that table on many occasions until ten o'clock at night with cold vegetables staring at me, and me trying to hide them under my knife and fork.

'You asked for those bloody peas, so you'd better bloody eat them'.

I also didn't know how to physically play with my peers. They would have rough and tumble games that I would try to join in with. But unfortunately, I didn't understand what was going on and often became too physical. By the age of 6 or 7, I was completely depressed. I was wetting the bed almost every night.

I wouldn't tell my mum and would sleep in the same bed covers until she changed them after a week. She would always say that it was because I was naughty and dreaming of naughty things. This continued for many years up to my teens.

I found school completely horrible. I would get up each morning filled with dread that I had to go to school. I would follow the same routine every morning but always tried to leave the house by myself and made sure not to find myself walking with anyone else.

I was bored in classes and never did any homework or anything that the teachers asked me to do. I was sent home with punishment exercises nearly every week which had to be signed by a parent. I had learnt to forge both my parents' signatures by this time.

The punishment was generally lines, such as writing, 'I must not talk in class' fifty times. It didn't take me long to create a device connecting ten pencils so that I could write fifty lines very quickly. Each pencil had to have a different weight attached to it so that the pressure was correct. Kids started paying me to do their lines for them. I would be happy when I saw someone getting lines because I knew they would pay me and I would go and buy cigarettes. I had started smoking by the age of 7.

I can't remember why, but I tried to kill myself for the first time when I was 7. I was so miserable that I took my bicycle lock and tied it around my bed and my neck. My mum came upstairs and found me hanging there. It was a combination lock and quite a sticky one, so it took her some time to get it off. She must have thought I had been mucking about because she just told me not to be so stupid, not to do it again and walked away.

After that failed attempt, I started to self-harm. I had quite a repertoire of techniques; one of them was trying to knock myself out by headbutting walls. I also learnt how to increase the blood pressure in my head to make myself pass out. I think a teacher must have spotted what I was doing and with my bad behaviour too, they finally called in a specialist to check me out.

An educational psychologist was brought into the school. She set me a series of questions over a few days and I actually enjoyed them. The questions gradually got more and more difficult and it felt good that I could answer them. It gave me a buzz working them out. Sometime later, my mum was called into school to hear what they thought about me.

What happened next really was a huge turning point in my life. The conversation that followed between the psychologist and my mum would have a profound impact on my life for many years into the future. Of course, I don't remember the full conversation, just this one part of it. The psychologist turned to my mum.

'You don't have to worry about him; he'll go straight to university'.

Bam! To say that to a parent who had already proved that she wasn't that bothered about her son was beyond comprehension. Now she had an excuse not to worry or care. My mum was told that I had an exceptionally high IQ and that they would be implementing a new teaching plan for me.

I was taken back to my classroom. A desk had already been put at the back of the class and on that desk was my very own edition of David Attenborough's Life on Earth. I loved that book and spent many hours reading it. The teacher told me to sit down.

'As you're so clever, study that', he said.

That was it, at 7 years old I was told to self-study. As I'm writing this today, I am horrified to think that professionals who were supposedly dedicated to the welfare, education and growth of children could act in such a way. To think that any of my children would be treated like this fills me with anger.

I have tried to get access to my school files but have been told that they were destroyed years ago. It would make very interesting reading. However, we must remember that this was the late 70s and early 80s so knowledge of developmental issues with children was very limited.

After this all happened, my self-harming intensified and I withdrew further and further into myself. I learnt that I could rub my ruler on the edge of the desk until it was red hot and burn my arms with it. I then found out that I didn't feel much pain in my arms, so I started experimenting by sticking needles through my skin.

Eventually, I was able to stick a long needle straight through my arm, although I do remember one time hitting something deep inside my arm other than the bone with which I was already familiar and screaming in pain. It must have been a nerve, so I didn't do it again for a few days after that.

I was smoking whatever I could get my hands on. I had no social circle. But I kept going to school; I kept functioning as I was expected to function, I suppose. The teacher knew there was something different about me as I remember one incident that they must have all planned together in the staff room to humiliate me.

I was asked to go to another classroom to collect a long stand so that my teacher could hang things on it. I think I was 8 years old at the time. This was quite an honour because it meant that you were trusted to leave the classroom and walk the school corridors on your own so I set off with my head held high.

As I walked into the classroom, I was met with 30 faces staring back at me. I remembered what I was there for so, in a confident voice, I asked the teacher for a long stand. The teacher smiled at me, picked up a piece of chalk, drew a big cross on the ground in front of the class.

'Stand there', he directed.

As I moved towards the cross, the whole class erupted in laughter. I was made to stand there until just before the end of class and then was sent back to my classroom. I don't need to tell you how that made me feel.

To think that the teachers must have been aware of how literal I was and that they must have all been laughing together in the staff room when they came up with the plan of how to humiliate me and how they must have laughed afterwards when their plan had worked, they had managed to fool the strange boy who sat by himself.

第二章

The whole night was spent in pain and delirium. All I needed to do was to get out and get one bag of number 4 and I would be fine. They could then put me back inside; I would be ready and prepared. Just one bag. I spent hours thinking about how I could get out. Feign illness? Escape?

People escape from prison, right? This place was run by stupid people, wasn't it? It would be easy to escape from them, from here. But the pain. The bed was a plain wooden plank and every part of my body that came in touch with it felt as if it was covered in bruises, from my head to my feet.

The stress was also causing my asthma to flare up. I knew that without my inhaler it would get worse. I had tricks which I had learned over the years that I could use to reduce the oncoming breathlessness, but I also knew that two puffs of an inhaler would immediately fix it.

I paused for a moment, weighing up my position and whether I had enough reason to push the small metal button on the cell wall near the bars at the front of my concrete room. I was already scared to do the wrong thing. Scared of breaking the rules this first night, not knowing what the punishment could be. Surrounded by all the unknown, I felt unsure.

I reached out and pushed the button. I stood there in the dark, straining my ears to listen to echoing sounds of a harsh, guttural language. Listening out for the sound of leather soles hitting the concrete floor, one after another, becoming louder which would signify the approach of a guard. But nobody came. I don't know how long I waited but after a good length of time, I decided that it had been long enough, so I pushed it again. I kept pushing it and pushing it.

That's what it was there for, wasn't it? Push it and surely they must have to come. I needed my inhaler. The panic started to rise again. Every so often, I would hear heavy footsteps coming down the corridor. I would get up as a guard walked past. I called out but they ignored me and continued walking.

They kept walking into the distance, then I would hear three clicks shortly followed by them walking back past. I pleaded again for help but they ignored me and kept walking. The footsteps faded into the distance again.

I had to breathe through my clothes to calm myself down. I needed the toilet in the night, the heroin-induced constipation I had not even acknowledged previously was now slowly undoing itself.

I quickly learnt that every sudden pain was no wind but a five-second warning to stumble through the dark and find the area in the back corner of the cell which I could only discern by its small step up to it. I had a second to guess if I was positioned correctly, barely caring if I was or not. Personal hygiene and worrying about making a mess were the furthest thoughts from my mind.

Those moments of internal relief, regular throughout that first evening, were so intense that they completely blocked out my surroundings. For those brief few seconds, I felt relief and not fear. At the end of the first, there was fear. One thing I was given before entering the cell was some thick, rough, pink toilet paper. Four squares to be exact, folded neatly. I had used them earlier to blow my nose, which was now running profusely, another new withdrawal symptom.

I had not thought of saving any. Who has ever run out of toilet paper? I remembered there was a sink to the left of the toilet so I reached out trying to find it in the dark. I was having a real problem trying to keep my balance, not being used to a hole in the ground toilet, whilst desperately trying to keep my splattered arse away from the trousers I had been given and was still wearing.

I managed to lean back against the wall as my legs started to go dead, providing me with what I believed was another ten or twenty more seconds to try and sort myself out. I found the sink and let my hand move up it and along the back until I found the tap. I had no idea how it worked, and it took the remaining seconds to finally discover that to use it I had to push the top down.

A small trickle of freezing water came out of the tap. I moved my hand to the water and, of course, it immediately stopped when I removed my hand from pushing down the top. The last five seconds started ticking loudly in my head. If I reached zero, I did not know what I would do.

I just felt a disaster looming, a disaster that may end with my trousers covered in shit and me having to sleep in them all night. That was too depressing to contemplate so with one last push, I stretched my fingers out so I could push the top and cup the water that came from the tap. I had never done this before so I was learning on the job.

I gathered a small amount and, grimacing, reached around to start cleaning myself. I felt sick doing this but I had to keep going. I managed to get one more small handful and cleaned myself enough so that I could now stand up and move to the sink itself. There I could use two hands to clean myself, which I did thoroughly. Now all I had to deal with was a wet arse, a cold wet arse.

Chapter Two

Eventually, I escaped primary school and moved to secondary. I remember being lost in the big school. Every break, I would find a corner of the playground and try to disappear into it.

Each lunchtime, I would go into the woods and smoke cigarettes by myself. Sometimes I would go home, but not often.

In my first year there, my English teacher asked me to stand up and read an extract from a book. Now, this I could do! I always prided myself on being the very best reader in class. I could scan way ahead of myself whilst reading so that my delivery was flawless. I was standing up in front of the class reading away very happily until I came to the word 'stork'.

I was born in England but we moved to Scotland when I was a baby so I didn't pick up an English accent. But I do have a different accent. I pronounce words differently from other people. The Scottish roll their Rs; I am not able to.

The teacher asked me to say the word again and again, and again. She got me to keep repeating it for what felt like fifteen minutes. I felt completely humiliated. At the end of the class, she sent me home with a punishment because she thought I was doing it on purpose. I gave it to my mum who just signed it and told me not to do it again!

Not long after that, I started drinking. I would go into my parents' drinks cabinet and fill a small bottle up with a bit of this and a bit of that. I would take my ill-gotten gains into the woods with my cigarettes and consume both. I would then stagger home and sneak up to my bedroom where I would engage in one of my hobbies.

Given my general lack of birthday presents, unusually I was given a fish tank one year. Within a couple of years, I had twenty. That was my main obsession for a long time. I would spend hours reading and learning everything possible about the fish I had.

I learnt their Latin names, where they came from, the acidity of the water they preferred and their breeding preferences. The first fish I was able to breed was Zebra Danios. I spent hours checking their water quality to ensure that everything was perfect. I ended up with a tank full of them.

I was devoted to the large fish tank that I had in the living room. In the first year, not one fish died, of which I was very proud. I had a perfectly balanced ecosystem, which fish perfectly balanced the other. My pride and joy were two silver dollars that were by now six inches in diameter.

I had almost lost one to a fungal infection that had attacked the whole side of its body. I tried isolating it and medicating the water but that didn't work. I reread my books and found one that gave me step-by-step instructions on how to operate on the fish. So, with needles, scalpels and scissors I set to work. It took some time, but I eventually managed to return the fish to the tank where it continued to thrive.

Months later, there was a large three-day fish contest in Glasgow. I took my two beautiful silver dollars along. They were kept in a tank together at my request. I went in each day and stayed with them for hours to monitor them. The contest was over three days. I knew I wouldn't win anything because one of them had a huge scar on its side, but I just really enjoyed showing them off as a proud parent. I went in every day to check on them.

On the third and final day, as I walked towards their tank, I couldn't believe what I was seeing. There was a big rosette on the tank. I had won best fish in the show by a junior, and I got a trophy for it too. I was so proud. Beaming, I went up to collect my trophy and then took my fish home again on the bus. Years later my parents threw out all my fish stuff including the trophy, but I still have one photo of them together.

School was becoming worse and worse for me. I had very little contact with anyone else there. The kids I did hang out with would be my friend one minute and then beat me up the next. I went home once after such a beating that my face was all over the place, only to be shouted at by my parents who told me to go and finish my paper round. They did ask me what happened to my face. I told them I was playing football and nothing else was mentioned.

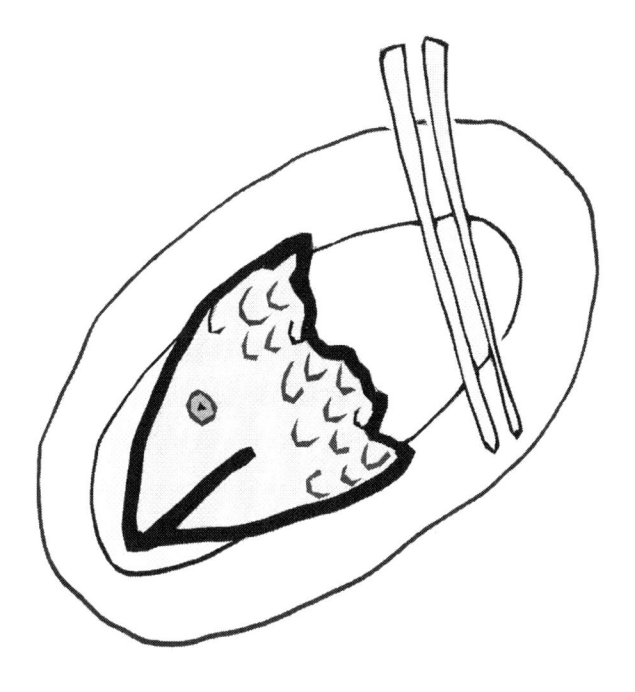

第三章

In my dreams, I was fighting. My friend Lennon and I had been jumped by another gang. There were five or six of them and we were outside the airport for some reason. Actors in a crazy kung fu movie, Lennon and I were standing back-to-back defeating anyone who got too close.

Then a gun came out and was pointed at my face. I brought my left hand around, up and out, knocking the firearm out of their hand. I stepped back and tripped over someone on the ground. Before I could get up, the gun was again pointed at my face.

BANG.

I was surrounded by a bright light. For a moment I felt warmth from the light but then an explosion of sound finally woke me from the vivid dream, bringing me physically back into the cell and the nightmare of my reality. I wasn't dead; I wouldn't die today. I had made it.

It was my 18th birthday.

The explosion of sound was a radio speaker in the corridor outside my cell with some Chinese guy shouting from it. It sounded like something from an old film, with some elderly Chinese guy yelling at his troops before they went into battle, waving their stupid red books. It went on and on. I had no idea what was going on. I tried to go back to sleep and pulled the horrible covers over my head. Then there was shouting which became louder as it came closer and closer to my cell. Along with it came a strange, loud metallic rattling noise. It stopped every so often and then a guard would start shouting.

I recognised my first bit of Chinese.

'Diu lay lo mo, chow hai' [fuck your mother, smelly cunt] repeated again and again. Then the rattling would begin again. It got to my cell. Whack! Right on the top of my head.

'Diu lay low mo, hai sun' [fuck your mother, get up].

My covers were pulled off. I jumped up. A guard was standing there, truncheon in hand. He had hit me with it; this was the noise I heard. He was running his truncheon along all the bars of the cells to get everyone up. I got up.

He shouted something at me and then walked away to the next cell.

I could now take in my cell properly. It could not have been cleaned in months or even years, it was filthy. I went to the toilet and nearly vomited. It was caked with shit, it stank of stale urine, all mine from my night-time adventures, I needed to go again. I stood over it, pulled my trousers down and tried to squat down. I could now see what I was doing and so I was able to hold onto the small concrete wall in front of me. I held on to it and did what I had to do.

It was not the most comfortable experience I had ever had; my knees were aching, and parts of my body were not as clean as I would have liked them to be. I reached over and was able to get the water I needed to clean myself.

I went to pull the small metal handle which stuck out from the wall and it just spun round in my hand. No flush. That is why the toilet was so bad. How was I going to live like this? I had just had a severe bout of the runs and I could not flush it away. I didn't even have any toilet paper.

I went to the sink to fill up my plastic cup with water to use to flush it. I pushed the tap, no water. Suddenly a huge thirst came on; I felt the panic building again. How could I survive this? I did not know how long I was going to be stuck here.

It was eerily quiet with only the guards shouting in the background. I lay back down on my bed. It was not for long. More shouting erupted at the end of my corridor. I got up and looked out. There were dirty windows on the other side of the corridor. They led out onto a rubbish-filled courtyard and, on the other side, were more windows leading to more corridors and cells. I could now, for the first time, get an idea of where I was.

A guard came to my cell, started to shout something and unlocked my door. I stood there for a moment not knowing what was going to happen next. I cautiously moved towards the open door like a frightened rabbit and poked my head outside.

I looked left and then right. All the other prisoners were leaving their cells, so I followed. As I stood outside my cell it felt like I was free again, but only for a fraction of a second. Then the guard returned shouting again and as I watched all the other guys turned and started walking towards the end of the corridor.

I fell into line like a robot already programmed for this event. We were led outside and made to stand two by two in a line. We were then marched away from the cell block. I had no idea what time it was. The whole place was covered in a thick layer of mist but this time it was light grey. It was freezing cold. Now and again, a wisp of wind would send the light grey cloud scurrying in different directions. The place looked like it went on forever. Through the veil of fog, I could occasionally see the outer wall.

A huge concrete structure with a round top came into view. As my eyes followed it around, I saw a watchtower. Standing on it was a guard with a large gun staring right back at me. I tried to follow the wall around but it disappeared into the mist. We finally reached another building where we were being led into, one by one. I managed to look through a window and saw it was full of prisoners in blue and brown uniforms.

I got into the building to find that it was a dining hall. There must have been five hundred prisoners inside. The blue uniforms were separated from the brown. We walked along the wall, one by one. There were shutters in the wall that were open by only five or six inches at the most. As I reached the first shutter, a yellow plastic mug was pushed out with a brown watery substance with brown twigs in it.

I picked it up and moved to the next shutter, a blue plastic plate emerged with a horror show all over it. A mound of white rice with two decapitated fish heads with congealed eyes staring back at me. I nearly threw the plate back but by the time I was able to process the vision in front of me, I had been pushed out of the line.

I was now following the line towards a table. The room was full of metal tables with three prisoners sitting on each side. The weird thing was that there was barely any sound apart from the slurping of rice off spoons. My table was at the back of the room. I sat down with the other prisoners and placed my plate and cup in front of me.

In amongst the horror of receiving the plate, I had not noticed the tray of chopsticks and spoons, so I had nothing to use to eat my breakfast. Not that it mattered; I had no appetite anyway. I just could not even consider eating anything. Everyone all around me was tucking into their food. In the middle of the table was a big blue bowl into which people were spitting the mashed-up remnants of fish heads.

I looked around across the horizon of black hair and, to my delight, saw a guy with brown hair. He was quite tall but walked hunched over. Just behind him was a shorter guy with blonde hair. They moved silently towards a table and sat down. They both had brown uniforms on. I felt like an alien wanting to contact one of my own. We made eye contact and there was a small nod from both then they turned around and got on with their breakfast. By this point, others were finishing their food and throwing their plates into the blue bowl in the middle. So, I grabbed my plate and did the same.

As the rice and fish slipped into the bowl, big groans erupted from everyone at my table. I had just committed my first obvious prison faux pas. If you do not want to eat, you should offer your food to others. There was nothing I could do at this stage and quite frankly, I could not have given a fuck. So I gave them all a look telling them to fuck off.

My withdrawals were kicking in again. It felt like all my orifices wanted to let go. Vomiting, shitting and pissing all felt like the right thing to do. Fortunately, my thoughts of painting the dining room floor were interrupted by a guard making us get up from the table and leave through a door that I had not noticed right behind us. I threw one last glance over my shoulder to the two foreigners that I had seen earlier hoping to catch their eyes. They felt like my salvation in this hell. I could communicate with them; they could help me survive.

We were taken back to the first building that I had been taken to the night before. I was too ill to care now. We went into the building one by one. It had been changed back to its original purpose, a doctor's waiting room with a couple of desks with prison officers in white coats. It was now that I realised that I had to be honest if I was going to survive.

I was called over to see one of the officers. I sat down and told him straight out that I was a heroin addict. That was the first time that I had admitted it to myself, let alone to anyone else. He laughed.

'Why didn't you tell us last night? Go and sit over there'. I went and sat in another seat. A while later, I was led through to another room where I saw an actual doctor. I sat down and went through my medical history with him. I was then led further up the corridor where there were cells.

A door on the left was opened and I was pushed inside. A guy there led me into a shower room. I was told to take off all my clothes and another guy came in with a hose. He turned it on and the water came out at full power. It was cold and stung so much that it nearly knocked me over.

He continued for what felt like ten minutes. I was then given a towel and told to dry myself. The guy with the hose then grabbed a bucket with a mug in it. The bucket was full of white powder and he started throwing it all over me. It was then that I noticed that he had gloves on. He made me rub the powder all over my whole body including my hair. I was being deloused.

I was told to sit on a chair in the shower room and wait. I stank of chemicals, it smelt like petrol. My skin started to itch; it was excruciating. After an hour, I was allowed to have a cold shower to get the dust off. I was given a white uniform to put on and was led out of the shower room into the cell.

It was the first time I was able to take in my surroundings. It looked like a hospital ward; well, it was a hospital ward. On the left were two low fibreglass beds with mattresses, white sheets and a pillow. The next three beds against the wall were actual hospital beds. On the right wall was one more hospital bed running along the wall to a table. Between each bed was a locker. I was given the second bed on the left. The guy who had been responsible for showering and delousing me was in the first bed.

I was later to find out that he was the head prisoner in the hospital. He was there because he was a child rapist and diabetic.

Then some of the other patients came over and sat down to speak with me. Only two of them spoke any English. The one who spoke the best English was a young guy called Danny. I say 'guy' but the reason he was in the hospital was because he was gay, breasts and all, manicured fingernails, plucked eyebrows, the works. He said he was not allowed to go to a hall in case he had sex with anyone.

They asked me about myself and it was then that I remembered that it was my 18th birthday. I told them and the guy sitting next to me went to his locker. He got out three boiled sweets and gave them to me.

'Happy birthday', he said.

It was the strangest thing. I was overwhelmed; it was the nicest thing that anyone had ever done for me up to that point in my life. Three treasured sweets given to a stranger. They left me to have them. I collapsed onto the bed. The next two weeks were going to be the worst of my life.

Chapter Three

I was heading towards the back gate of school one fine day when I heard a lot of footsteps behind me. They weren't walking but running. I turned around and there was Alex. I had known this guy my whole life. He was a wee guy but a very fast runner and good at football.

We had been friends at different times of our lives but since secondary we had become distant. Anytime I met him we would always interact as good friends if he was alone.

It's funny, he's probably one of the guys I would have done anything for. I would have helped him and supported him anywhere, anytime. He did have an aggression about him I don't know exactly why, possibly family stuff and the fact that he was shorter than the rest.

Anyway, something had made him hostile. He came up to me and said those immortal words of the Scottish playground. The word that I had heard said to me, was the word that I had chanted on many occasions when I wasn't involved. The word that could send shivers up and down your spine.

'Fight!'

I looked around me; the crowd had drawn a circle around the combatants. In their eyes a hunger for action and a grateful expression that they weren't involved. I looked at Speedy, as that was his nickname, and realised that I didn't want to fight him.

This was for a few reasons. First, I was worried that I could hurt him; I didn't want to. My reach was so much longer than his and I must have weighed at least half more than his weight. He was an old friend; I liked him. The fight would be unfair, I knew he was fast, but I had been smashed so many times in the face and body that I tended to be able to take even the biggest hits. I said to him that I didn't want to fight but he just said it again.

'Fight!'

He pushed me, I just stood there. He pushed me repeatedly, I just stood there. The crowds were getting louder, and the numbers were building as others heard the playground jungle drums.

'Fight, fight, fight!'

He then went to punch me. I had to think about what to do, where to hit him. I needed to put him down with the least damage to him possible. I wanted it to end quickly so that he would be okay.

I took a load of his hits and then found my moment when I swung with my left fist hard into the underside of his right lower jaw. I knew this was a good place to jar the vestibular system and cause a knockout.

I connected beautifully but not beautifully enough. Although he was sent flying to the ground, he was helped up and ran at me again, fists flailing.

Okay, I thought, maybe not as easy as I hoped. What to do next? All this whilst fending off blows and holding him back. He was getting tired so I decided to give him a huge jab to the diaphragm to wind him with my left and then a big uppercut right under his chin.

The second punch was not needed as the body blow sent him flying, gasping for the air that had been ripped out of him. As if in slow motion, I was realising that this was the end of the fight. I would be able to walk away and get on with my day.

He was lying on the ground and I moved towards him to help him up. I had no bad feelings towards him and I was just saying sorry when I was grabbed from behind. It was the first time in my life that I had gone flying backwards because someone had grabbed me. It was a weird experience as well as incapacitating as there is no way of countering it at all.

As my back slammed into the ground ten black school shoes came flying towards me. I was getting pummelled by the initial group that had joined Speedy in the beginning. It was a total set-up. No matter what happened they had planned for me to get a total kicking. For what purpose? I still really haven't a clue. Presumably for kicks and power.

This wasn't the first time I had been set up and it was not the last either. It had previously happened on a scouting trip when the older lads made me fight a smaller guy. I had refused but they made me do it and then kicked the shit out of me because I had won that fight too. I knew I had to get out of there, with or without my dignity.

One well-aimed boot could have ended it all. They weren't trying to kill me, but it could happen. Did anyone have a knife? I was out of there in five seconds, throwing them all back and legging it out of the school. No one followed me; I was alone. I had escaped. I would never go back. I would never see most of them again

第四章

Everything that had happened to me in the past eighteen years would be nothing compared to the two weeks of withdrawing from the strongest heroin on the planet.

For the first couple of days, it did not matter where I was, prison, home or on the streets, my whole miserable existence consisted of my bed and the toilet if I even made it there. I generally did not.

No matter how I lay on my bed, I could not get comfortable. Every part of my body that had weight put on it screamed in agony. I would wet myself and shit myself constantly. The diarrhoea was the worst. If I did manage to fall asleep, I would wake up with my clothes and bed covered in shit.

Twice a day, a senior prison officer would come around to inspect the hospital. Each time he came around, we had to stand up next to our bed. The hospital guard would shout something, to which everyone would respond,

'No sir.'

The senior officer would look around and then leave. On more than one occasion, when this happened, I passed out and found myself lying on the floor somewhere. I was constantly sneezing as if I had the worst flu in history. I had no appetite and would throw up anytime I tried to eat.

I received no medication, and no help at all from the hospital staff or doctor. A couple of prisoners helped me with water and helped themselves to my food. I could not eat it, so they might as well.

On the third day, I started to become more aware of my surroundings. I was in a hospital ward with six other prisoners, five beds with their heads against one wall, and another lengthways on the other side with its end coming up against a communal table where the others sat and ate their food. This was where the two gay guys would also sit during the day as they were not allowed in the general population, homosexual activity was taboo.

There was a small TV high on the wall that I could remember hearing in the distance when I was delirious. At the other end of the ward, past the barred door, there was the toilet. Unlike what I had witnessed my first night which was just a hole in the ground, there were two cubicles with actual sitting toilets. There were also showers, this was where all new patients were given the cold hose pipe treatment and then deloused.

Across from our ward, there were two other single cells. They were in constant use; a continuous stream of new inhabitants would be locked inside only to be removed and replaced by someone else. These were segregation cells for the more difficult prisoners. Not punishment cells but where mentally ill people were placed.

Prisoners who were a danger to others and themselves. Serious self-harmers who would rip themselves to pieces if given the chance. They were suicide watch cells where prisoners could be monitored and kept safe.

This is when I learnt a new sound and what it always meant. I missed it the first time it happened when I was there but, not to worry, it would happen regularly enough for me to instantly wake from my sleep and know that someone had decided that enough was enough.

That first time, all I knew was that the guy next to me was out of his bed and calling for the night officer because it always happened when the prison was at its quietest in the middle of the night.

I was still a bit delirious but I knew something was not right. There was a lot of shouting, then quiet when the guard went away. Then a lot of noise again when the clatter of many rubber-soled boots came running up the narrow corridor.

The noise of keys rattling in the lock, some more shouting, things being moved, and then as if all moving as one, the noise slowly moved back down the corridor and faded away. The next morning the cell was empty, waiting for its next inhabitant.

I did not have to wait long for it to happen again, and this time I heard it and understood. All the cell furniture was made of fibreglass: the stools to sit on, the table to eat on and the beds to sleep on. The floors were all concrete, just like the walls and ceilings. When moving any of the fibreglass items to sit on or whilst cleaning, they always made the same distinctive noise against the concrete floor.

It was always the same tone, only the volume would either increase or decrease. It was not a pleasant sound, like nails down a blackboard, so it was one that we all tried to avoid making.

The sound that happened at night, the same fibreglass against concrete was different and it always meant the same thing. It was a sound that you could not replicate by accident. It only happened when someone had tied something around their neck and attached the other end to the very top of their cell door by standing on their stool.

It was the sound of the stool being forcibly pushed away from under them, the thin legs scraping along the concrete, but with their weight and force added to it, then the top of the stool hitting the ground.

That was it, that was the hanging sound, it happened a lot. If done at night, it was never just a cry for help. I would learn this over time, we all became experts in the many ways in which it was carried out. It was day five or day six that this new life experience would offer itself up again to me.

There was not one night that I slept peacefully. Each night was different: sweats, pain, soiling myself, nightmares. But so far, I had been so deep in delirium that nothing managed to get through to me and catch my attention. That night, it was all going to change.

It was deathly silent. I was lying in my bed listening to the silence, trying to catch the slightest sound. There, I heard something, the sound of movement, a movement purposely made and made quietly. I sat up a little in bed, my eyes wide now, my ears trying to locate where it came from. It went quiet for a few moments, nothing. Then scrape, bang.

Chapter Four

I ran straight from school to the train station where I got the train into Glasgow and found the Royal Navy's recruitment office. Joining or running away, the definition didn't matter.

It wasn't quite as easy as that of course. I had to sit a lot of tests and be interviewed. The tests reminded me of the ones I had done when I was 7 and I found them even easier than before. I was then sent home with something for my mum to sign as I was only 16. She signed it without saying much and that was it.

A few weeks later, I headed off to England, down to HMS Raleigh in Plymouth by train and started what was to be, up until then, the most stressful but, in hindsight, easy six months of my life.

You would have thought that the Navy would have been the worst possible place for a person with Asperger Syndrome, an Aspie, to be, but you'd be wrong. Routine, routine, routine. It was great. I knew where I was going, what I was doing, when I slept and when I had to wake up. It was heaven. The difficult part was the other people.

I thought I was crazy. The Navy was full of dropouts, 'Can't make it in the real world, join the Navy' should have been their advertising campaign. It was all about teamwork. Teamwork whilst we were doing something work-related and intense was okay for me but when you returned to your dorm and people were hanging out together, I just couldn't hack it.

My first home leave was coming up and I wouldn't have anywhere to go as I couldn't head to Hong Kong where my parents and younger brother were now living. I asked if I could stay on base but my request was refused and I was told to go home. So, off I trundled a few weeks later back to Glasgow where my older brother was now living with his girlfriend in the house. He had decided to stay when my mum and dad and wee brother moved.

I got there and nobody was home so, for the first four hours of home leave I was sitting on the front step waiting for my brother. When he did get back and let me in, I went up to my bedroom which was now a dumping ground for all his stuff. No room at the inn. So, I decided to sleep in the garage. I was glad to leave a week later to go back down to Plymouth.

Our passing out parade was coming up which is when you all dress in your finest uniform and march in front of dignitaries and family and friends to celebrate the completion of basic training. During the run-up to the parade, I had a series of stress-related incidents.

The first was waking up in the morning completely blind. I lay on my bed for what seemed like an eternity trying to decide whether I was awake or still asleep and whether I was going to be blind forever. Eventually, my sight came back but it was very scary.

The next thing was my right knee freezing. I couldn't straighten it. For that, I had to go to the medical staff who put me on restricted duties for a week, so that ended the possibility of me passing out with everyone else, although it didn't stop me from taking part in the passing-out parade.

Afterwards, I decided that enough was enough and put in a PVR, premature voluntary release request. They couldn't stop me from leaving as I was still only a kid, so off I went back to Glasgow. I did not stay with my brother so couch surfed for a couple of weeks until my parents agreed to put me on a flight to Hong Kong.

第5章

No sleep, no rest, feeling like it's a long journey of dying. Sweating, aching, delusional. Dreams are real. Fluids leaking from every hole from top to bottom. You have the same power to stop your arse running as you do your nose, none. Sneezing constantly, each time waking from feverish semi-consciousness finding yourself covered in shit. Wanting to die, sometimes pleading loudly for it to end. Eating or drinking feels irrational, why put anything else in when it causes pain and suffering until it eventually just ends up exiting at will?

One bag would cure it all, just one bag. Then I would stop; I promised everyone in the room.

A massive twisting pain in my stomach woke me up. Dizzy and confused with fever, I desperately tried to find the way to the toilet without tripping over anything. I was not quick enough and before I could reach the object of my desire, I felt myself letting go. But this time it was different; I had ejected everything I had and was now at the mucous stage.

I cleaned myself and had just got back to bed looking forward to some more sleep when the radio came on and the terrifying Chinese words that were barked repeatedly every day.

I managed to sit at the table and eat some of my bread and cheese. Becoming more aware of my surroundings now as my fever was starting to lift but I was still feeling very unwell. When I stood up from the table everything went dark. I had no idea how long I was out, but I woke up in bed to someone shouting, '27343 chit saam'. Then louder, 'Gwai Gi chit saam'. Someone pushed my shoulder, 'Gwai Gi, hai sun'

Just as I remembered that I was 27343 and Gwai Gi, I found myself flying but only for a second before I hit the ground. I opened my eyes to see a guard standing over me angrily shouting, 'Diu lay low mo Gwai Gi hai sun chit saam'. That is when I vomited all over myself.

The guard shouted something else to somebody else and I felt myself being pulled up and pushed into the shower room. The shower turning on was enough of a clue that I had to take my vomit, piss and shit-stained clothes off. The water was freezing and the soap was harsh. I washed as best I could. The water went off and fresh clothes were thrown at me. Trying to keep them as much out of the water on the ground as I put them on, failing miserably so now wearing wet clothes, I was pushed by the orderly towards the cell door and down the corridor to the waiting area where I had last been what felt like weeks previously. I collapsed on the wooden bench next to some surprised-looking Chinese guys who may have never seen a white guy before and not one looking as ill as I did.

Another guard came into the room and shouted, '27343'. This time I knew it was me and I stood up. He turned and walked out of the room so I followed. Outside there was a line of other prisoners so I joined the end of the line and we then were on our way following each other. I had no idea where I was going, but what other choice did I have?

We did not go far; it was only to the next building to the left of the main gate. I tried to have a look around but was quickly moved inside before I could get a good look at anything. My eyes found it difficult to focus on anything as I had only seen a 3 or 4-metre distance at the most recently. Anything beyond that was a blur, a painful blur. I was taken down a short corridor and into a room where I was handcuffed to a small metal table that was bolted to the ground. One part of the handcuff was attached to a leg and the other to my left wrist. I was told to sit on a rigid plastic chair which cut painfully into the skin at my hips. I put my arms on the table but immediately removed them as it was cold. I was shivering now, I only had thin white hospital pyjamas on and it was still early January. The door was shut behind me so I just sat there trying to keep warm, shivering with my nose running.

The door eventually opened and two large guys in suits walked in. They showed me their ID cards but, to be honest, I was so ill I was oblivious to what they were saying. They spent the next hour asking me questions, shouting at me, pushing me. Some of the stuff I knew but much of it I did not. My answers were vague and this did not please them. At one point, one of them started screaming at me, calling me a liar and scum, threatening me that I would never see my family again, would never leave there, and would die here unless I told them everything. My shrugging of the shoulders was enough to send him into a rage so he jumped up screaming at me and kicked my chair away from me. As I hit the floor, he kicked me in the guts. The floor was hard concrete, it was like a block of ice. I burst into tears, all my strength leaving me, and I curled up like a baby. They shouted a few more things as I lay there and then they left.

After the door closed, I lay there for a few more minutes until my tears stopped. I sat up and, slipping the handcuffs up the table leg with my left hand, I pulled the chair up with my right. I sat there for a while longer before the guard came in again, unlocked my wrist and gestured for me to follow him. For a moment I thought I felt some level of care from the guard, he was not as cold to me as he was when he first brought me over. With only me now, he led me back to the hospital and handed me back over. I walked straight back to the cell and lay down on my bed. No one said anything to me. I pulled my covers over me and used them to wipe my tears away.

fter lunch, my number was called again. This time, I was thrown the blue remand prisoner uniform to wear. I sat in the waiting room before being escorted to the building on the right, the reception room where I had gone that first night after being stripped and humiliated. I was told to sit on the benches, then my number was called again. I was getting used to it now, so I stood up and went to the guard who called me. He had a set of huge medieval-looking handcuffs which he attached to both of my wrists. He then attached the usual thinner handcuffs to my ankles and put a chain around my waist where another chin was attached to my ankles. The chain was short, obviously made for shorter guys so when I was told to follow him, I could not straighten up and had to walk with my back hunched over, which was anything but comfortable.

He took me to the visiting area where I had been that morning and I was put into an identical room as before. Once again, I waited for a few minutes when two police officers came in. They could have been the same ones from that morning but I could not tell. I thought they were but I was not sure. What was definite was that they did not like me and treated me like shit.

I was put in a van and driven somewhere. I had no idea what was going on. The clothes that I was arrested in were in a bag next to me and I was told to put them on. They were stinking and filthy. I looked terrible; I had not washed in days and had not shaved in a couple of weeks. I stank of all sorts, particularly urine and shit. I found myself being pushed into a lineup with maybe five other white guys. They all looked smart, cleanly shaven and hair done. I stood out like the proverbial sore thumb. They did allow me one concession and that was to choose where to stand in the line-up. God knows what these other guys thought when they were looking at me.

Anyway, almost immediately this Chinese guy was brought in to see if he could pick me out of the line-up. You would have had to have been thick not to see which one of us had been arrested recently. He picked me out straight away. Then another guy was brought in. Interestingly, he did not pick me out but when he was leaving, turned to a police officer and said he thought it was me. I did not stand much of a chance, no lawyer, looking like shit. I bet if I had been given the chance to shave and wear some nice clothes, I would not have been picked out. All of us Gwai Gi's look the same to the Chinese, don't we?

As soon as he was out of the door and before the other white guys had been led outside, the two officers came into the line-up room and immediately put the handcuffs and ankle chains back on me. I couldn't have been more embarrassed than if I had been standing there naked.

They took me out of the room, down a short corridor and then into another room. The guy in there almost jumped out of his skin when we entered. He was standing behind a camera and said something in Chinese to the officers who pushed me to sit on a seat directly in front of the camera. Once again, I had no idea what was going on but before I could even think, I looked up at the camera and it flashed twice. Then I was once again pulled to my feet and dragged back to the original holding cage where the chains and cuffs were removed and I was motioned to strip and put my blue prison uniform back on again.

I sat back down on the wooden bench in the cage and tried to get comfy with my back against the bars, it wasn't possible, so I found the least painful position and dozed off.

Sometime later, shouting woke me from my painful sleep. It took me a few moments to register that they were shouting at me but when the cage opened, the two officers grabbed me and started snapping the cuffs and chains back onto me. This time I winced when they were attached as they had started to cause bruising where they encountered my withered flesh. I shuffled painfully down the corridors and out into the car park where I was pushed into the van and we drove back towards the prison.

Chapter Five

'So, you want me to steal Graeme's car, drive you to the Halfway House restaurant at Symington, which is about 30 miles away, at midnight, to pick up your wallet which you left there the other night when you were having dinner with your parents, is that what you're asking me?'

With a smile, Gary said 'Yep'.

It is important to point out at this point that Gary and I were not known for this type of behaviour. I can safely say that neither of us had ever considered this kind of activity previously.

I had only recently started hanging out with Gary. It was just over a year that we had started spending most of our time together. I had known him longer; it was through our mutual friend Wendy that we had met. They had a short relationship. Then after they broke up, he started seeing a lassie called Helen, sweet smelling Helen, we called her.

We were at Gary's parents' place in Newton Mearns. I sat there thinking. 'Okay [I said] but if I am going to drive that far I need to at least practise driving the car, how do you think we can manage that? Graeme would never let us drive his car, it's a Merc'. 'I've got a plan', he said.

Now, planning was not our strongest capability. Even with both our heads together, we had produced a couple of the stupidest ideas ever.

We met when we were both 15. Just before my 16th birthday, I think. Gary was always skint so he would come up with ideas on how to make money.

His dad was in the music business before he retired. He was a much-loved personality throughout Glasgow. So, there was a room full of vinyl records in their house. The collection was huge as his dad would get a copy of every single that was in the charts.

One Saturday, we headed into the city centre with a pile of these records. It was Gary's idea to tie them up into bundles of five with a good one at the top and bottom and three rubbish ones in the middle. Criminal masterminds. He was the man with the plan, I was the man with sales banter. It just came naturally to me.

Gary was always worried that if the police came, they would ask his name and then they would find out who his dad was. So, when they did eventually come, I took it upon myself to banter us out of it, telling Gary to shut up and let me deal with it. It worked and we got away with a stern word and around £50 for a couple of hours of work.

We then carried out one of the dumbest things I have ever been a part of. Gary needed money again, so came up with another grand plan. We would get up early and go to a local newsagent, wait for the daily papers to be dropped off, which was usually around 6.00 am, grab a pile of the most expensive papers, go into the city centre and sell them on a corner just like a couple of paper boys. Easy.

I got up at 5.00 am, crept downstairs and got on my bike. It was always me who had to cycle to his house. No-one ever wanted to come to my house. I cycled over to Gary's which was a couple of miles away and all uphill. I met him at the corner of Kirkview Crescent then we headed towards the Harvie Avenue shop, all downhill thankfully.

Attempting to look as innocent as possible we sat on the curb of the car park and waited. What we did not realise was that there would be lots of people around. We stupidly thought that no-one would be around that early, but we were wrong.

'We'll be seen', Gary said worriedly.

'Probably, but if we just act completely naturally, they will think we're just paper boys, but we've got to act as if what we are doing is normal.

'We're going to get caught and my dad will kill me'.

I had already invested so much into this plan that I was going ahead with it whatever happened. Just as I turned to him the delivery van came into the car park and parked right next to us.

'Let's just go now', he said.

'Be cool, stay where you are, stop looking around, just wait and calm down', I replied.

It was not the heist of the century but for us it was intense. The adrenaline was pumping through us like neither of us had experienced before. This was quite audacious, in full view of people, with no hiding places, we were maturing slowly into quite the young villains. The papers were out, the van doors shut and the van was gone.

I stood up, walked over to the neat piles of Saturday morning reading and quickly found my target. The Glasgow Herald, 50p per copy. I grabbed a pile, shit!! A slight miscalculation, the pile weighed a tonne!

Of course, there was no Google back in the late 80s. I don't know if we would have even bothered to check anyway because we were such idiots. But a quick search now will tell you that a single inch of newspaper weighs 1.3 kg. I had grabbed a pile of at least 12 inches, 15.87 kgs.

The plan was then to take the papers back to my house where we would leave our bikes and then walk the mile to Patterton Station to get the train into Glasgow Central where we would find somewhere with a high footfall to sell the papers.

It must have been a hilarious sight, the two of us humping that heavy load. We made it and managed to sell quite a few before we were once again chased off by the police.

Those first two successes made us feel invincible. Invincible enough to think we would easily get away with stealing our friend's 300 E-class Mercedes and driving it over 60 miles on a road renowned for its high number of accidents. I should point out that neither of us had ever driven before.

Both Gary and Graeme smoked hash, I did not. I enjoyed my vodka and that was it. That was honed from years of having alcoholic parents who loved their spirits and me filling up different empty bottles with mixtures from their drinks cupboard. I did smoke cigarettes and had done since I was about 8 or 9.

My father worked overseas so would always come back with cartons of Benson and Hedges. He was never home long enough to smoke all that he brought with him so the cupboard in the kitchen where he kept them was always full of cartons, making it easy for me to take one without anyone knowing.

Gary planned to get Graeme so wasted that he would pass out. He regularly did that anyway. We spent most nights at his flat in Shawlands and it was his routine to disappear into his room around 11.00 pm and not reappear again until the morning, with the bonus that he never got up during the night. For a few nights, Gary and I checked that this was the case. We would wait for him to go to bed then wait different lengths of time before one of us would go in and try to wake him. He slept through it every time; we were sure of our plan.

After a night of getting Graeme as wasted as possible, we got hold of his car keys from where we had casually tossed them earlier and headed downstairs to the car park.

For the next hour, we drove the automatic Mercedes around the empty streets of Shawlands. I was so nervous, I half kept my foot on the brakes as I was driving. That ended when we came up to a set of traffic lights outside the Victoria Infirmary Hospital when Gary noticed smoke coming from the front of the car. We both jumped out to find the wheels glowing orange. There was nothing else to do but to drive the car back to the apartment without using the brakes.

As soon as I parked the car, I realised there was no way I could drive the car again but Gary had other ideas. 'Brilliant, so we'll do it on Saturday'. Being easily led, I simply nodded and that was it.

第6章

During those first two weeks, I was visited by my family for the first and what also happened to be the last time. I was taken to the reception, made to put on the blue uniform again and marched to the visiting room. It was a long narrow corridor with booths separated by concrete walls. In each booth, there was a stone seat and a thick steel-reinforced glass with a speaker and microphone built into the side of the wall. I waited for a couple of minutes sitting painfully on the stone and then in they came. My mum, dad and wee brother.

My mum sat down on their side and picked up a telephone next to her. She did not look good. Dad just stood behind her angrily not looking at me and my brother stood next to my mum. I must have looked terrible to them. The mundane questions came.

'How are you, how is the food?'

'Shit', I answered, 'Shit'.

Then came the news that they had decided to move back to the UK. They had met my court-appointed lawyer briefly, whom I had not even met yet and he said that he would keep them in the loop with what was happening. My mum said that she would write as often as she could. I asked if she could send me the addresses of my friends as I did not have any of their info with me and that they may be wondering what happened to me. She said that she would rather not and added

'Let's just see what happens'.

They asked me if I had seen my lawyer yet, I said no and that was that. When they got up to leave, I had no idea when or if I would ever see them again.

Back in the hospital, although in a deranged withdrawing state, I was aware of some things going on around me. The rapist next to me would do fifty push-ups about ten times a night at the same speed that you could count to fifty, right down and up, proper push-ups. The problem was that this was all he did and his upper body shape showed it. His upper back looked like he had twin humps and his chest looked like it had been pumped up with air.

Thinking that this child rapist was stronger now, stronger than before he came into prison, also made me quiver. This was all new to me and I was going through severe withdrawals. At times I wondered why I didn't beat him up for what he had done but I came to realise that this was the prison hierarchy.

You judge others so that you feel better about your crimes. The murderers had a hierarchy. Killing someone in a fight is okay but killing a granny whilst robbing her is worse. Killing an adult is better than killing a child. Kill a police officer and you are the top man. Rapists also have a warped hierarchy too. Raping a woman in the same age bracket as you are better than raping someone younger. For example, a 20-year-old raping a 19-year-old was better than a 50-year-old raping the same 19-year-old. Raping a grandmother was not as bad as raping a child.

But please do not think that the prisoners who have committed such grave crimes go around having competitions with themselves. This is simply not the case. They tend not to discuss it. They are category A prisoners and are held at the top of the prison hierarchy anyway because of their length of sentence. The lower-category prisoners were a different story. They were constantly trying to gain the respect of others to ensure their safety in prison. The ones who did not talk were the ones who had mugged grannies or thieves. Thieves were one of the lowest regarded prisoners. They were looked on with contempt, thought not to belong in prison because their crime was so pathetic.

Chapter Six

I sensed the start of the descent rather than feeling it. The tone of the engines changed; there was a slight change in the angle of the plane. It had been fifteen hours, this flight from Heathrow. I had sat there most of the trip not moving. I had done the usual check of the pocket in the seat back pocket and slipped the aircraft's magazine out first.

It had its usual typical stories of places of interest. Interest only in the destinations which the airline flew to. I don't think I'd ever read about a place in an airline magazine that the airline didn't fly to. Although I was only 16, I had been on a lot of planes. I then took out the complimentary headphones, plugged them into the armrest and listened to some radio but it was too much of a distraction. I needed to be alert, there was so much going on around me.

I had a window seat, which can be good and bad if you are anything like me. It's good because you have two angles at which you can put your head, not just the one if you are in the middle seat. The first angle is straight ahead. It doesn't give you much to look at apart from the person in front of you and if that's an annoying kid who then starts to think you are playing a game with them and peeking their 'oh so cute face' between the seats and over the top at you, you are in trouble.

If you are behind a chair recliner, well, you are fucked because then you're looking very closely at an airline headrest. This is not a clever idea because it is only then that you start to notice how disgusting the plane is.

You notice hairs on the coloured napkin thing on the seat rest that don't match the person sitting there. You realise that they do not get changed after each flight, and then you start to take in more.

Your senses go into overdrive. Not only is your hearing stretched to breaking point because you are listening to every creak of the aircraft's structure and the hum of the engines -- because in your world you are an aviation expert and the slightest change in engine hum means definite disaster -- and listening to every conversation around you because when you open your hearing up to the plane, you can't then turn off the background chatter. You are also listening to the bells or buzzers that tell the cabin crew what the pilot is up to, et cetera.

Then you start going into breakdown mode. You are looking for dirt and grime and you start seeing it but you also realise that the interior of the aircraft isn't as well maintained as you thought it should be. You start to wonder if that loose panel just to the front and right of you, above the overhead lockers, could contribute to the overall destruction of the aircraft. Then there's a bit of turbulence and you see the panels moving. Oh shit, they're not secure! The gap starts to open and you hear a bell ping twice, that must mean trouble, no seat belt sign, why? Why? The pilot hasn't had time to put it on and then another bump. Shit, the port engine has changed, it's about to explode!

Then you start to smell things too. It's strange because I thought you couldn't smell anything on a plane. You can but it's just a little bit more difficult. I find myself doing some sniffing, and some more sniffing, but then I stop as it sounds like I've got a cold and there is nothing worse than sitting next to someone on a plane who's got a cold. Your nose starts to run, you feel a sneeze coming.

'I will not sneeze, I will not sneeze, I will not blow my nose because that's me admitting I've got a cold or the flu!'

You wipe your nose, secretly -- don't let anyone see you -- and look the other way, impossible if you're in the middle seat as there is no other way and the glare of two strangers from both sides would be felt. But I'm at the window. So, I turn to the window and lower my head into my left hand as if resting, all the time listening to hear if anyone is talking about my sniffing. Then, when the coast is clear, I wipe my finger across my nose. Damn, I didn't get it all and now I feel a sneeze coming. So, I lower my head more until my nose is now resting on my hand. I squeeze it secretly between my fingers to stop the sneeze, 'Shit, more snot'.

I wipe my nose and hold it at the same time to stop the sneeze. I do anything not to sneeze and we all know that just makes it worse! Eventually, I must do the inevitable and go to the bathroom before I have a sneezing fit. I try to start pumping adrenaline around my body to give me the strength to ask my two neighbours to excuse me. When I've mustered up the strength, I turn to the first one to find the fucker asleep

I have to decide whether to wake them up and try to squeeze by them but then I run the risk of waking them up in a startling way. If I wake them up first, they will have to stay awake until I get back from the toilet, thus limiting the time I have in the toilet. Just because I need to blow my nose doesn't mean that I shouldn't make use of this rare opportunity to do all the normal toileting activities: pee, shit, face wash, check for spots, washing pits also a possibility.

Then the next thing to be checked is whether the person in front of my neighbour is an annoying seat recliner. If they are, I have to make sure that when I go past and put my hand on their chair for leverage, I don't pull their hair. I've done it before and I've had it done to me; not fun.

I make it to the aisle with the minimum fuss. Shit, I now remember that I had sensed the plane descending. Any minute now, the fasten seat belt sign will go on. I look around to see that people are looking at me; if I give the game away, they'll all be up. Look cool, relaxed…shit a sneeze that won't go away. It's coming! My nose is dripping, well at least it feels like it is.

I must look like I'm going to throw up, I really have to sneeze. I need to get my hand to my face quickly! Another dilemma, especially when being watched. If it's not too bumpy, easily done but if there's turbulence and you try to walk down without holding on, you know you're going to land in someone's lap. Oh, the pressure. Somehow, I make it. Nose, bladder, bowels emptied. Hands, face and armpits washed. Paper towels discarded in the correct receptacles.

Should I wipe down the toilet seat after use, as theM signage requests, for the comfort of the next passenger?

Back in my seat, I look out of the window, it's cloudy with a few breaks. The captain comes on. 'Nice to have been your captain yah, it's now time for me to perform a skill all of you think I must be a superhero to perform. Love to you all. God bless the queen'. I look out of the window and the fasten seat belt sign goes on. We descend through the first layer of cloud, smooth as silk.

I had never been here before. I was staring out of the aircraft window, trying to get my first glimpse of the place. I hadn't physically been here, but I had dreamt about it. My parents and younger brother had moved here about a year ago, I hadn't seen them since.

Two years ago, I had a dream. My mum came into my room one morning and said she had something to tell me. I said, 'I know, we're moving to either Manchester [I was a Man Utd fan] or Hong Kong. She just stared at me for a moment and then said, 'We're moving to Hong Kong'. She didn't ask me how I knew, nothing more was said about it. It hadn't ever been mentioned before. She must have got a late-night call from my dad telling her that his company was promoting him and that meant an office job in Hong Kong.

Through the clouds, I got my first glimpse. It was a Chinese junk boat in full sail; it was beautiful, right down there on the vast ocean. Then we were in the clouds again and it was gone.

I had flown many times before, between two and four times every year for holidays as well as from Somerset to Glasgow just after I was born but what happened next scared the shit out of me. I was used to wee turns left and right on a plane, but this was different. The whole aircraft violently turned to the right. We were virtually on the wingtips. My whole body stiffened, the vice-like grip of anxiety gripped my stomach and my chest felt like an elephant was sitting on it, my sphincter grabbed on for dear life. But I had experienced some turbulence before, so I assessed the situation.

Everyone else was calm. There was no look of worry or panic on anyone's face, no screaming apart from in my head, no announcement to take up the brace position. By the time I had gone through my checklist, the plane righted itself and then the most amazing sight came into view.

High-rise buildings. We were flying right past high-rise buildings. Not past them but through the middle of them. I could see washing hanging on lines, air conditioner units strapped to the side of them like some sort of futuristic parasite. Then I could see people in their flats. It all whipped past quickly, we were in a 747 after all, but I could see it. Then as we descended even more, I was looking at a grey scene, a concrete jungle. Then we were down. That was crazy, I thought to myself.

After disembarking, I followed the crowd and retrieved my luggage. My family was going to be there, weren't they? I didn't have much money, only what was left from my last wage from the Navy, but I did have their address on Conduit Road Mid-Levels, so I knew I could get there if I had to. It was then that I noticed that I was starting to shiver, the air-conditioning was crazy.

I had left a chilly Scotland in October and arrived in a roasting Hong Kong. I remembered that when we got off the plane it was sweltering but now the air-conditioning in the arrivals hall was starting to send me into some sort of shock.

I followed the crowd. We came to some big sliding doors that opened automatically on approach onto a downward slope with railings on either side and people hanging onto eagerly waiting loved ones, or not. The arrivals hall.

I saw the familiar faces of my family. Well, not all of them of course. My older brother had elected to stay in Scotland and by the looks of it, my dad had elected not to be there. Not that I thought he would be there of course. Firstly, I had left his beloved Navy after just 6 months, I had quit. I didn't get on with it in the end. I did everything that I was supposed to do, passed everything and even got an exceptional commendation sent to my mum, which I never saw. But I just didn't get on with it. Anyway, my father was never generally there anyway.

My wee brother and my mum were there to greet me. Hugs and stuff followed and then they led me outside. The heat hit me like a blast furnace. Air conditioning is good until you go outside and then you realise that some idiot had had it on too cold. We headed towards a long taxi queue and stood in line. My mum and my brother were asking me a lot of questions but I was just trying to take it all in. I looked about. We got into a red taxi, just like a New York taxi but red. I clambered into the front seat and used the only Cantonese I had learnt, 'Nei ho ma' [How are you].

The driver replied. He could have called me a prick for all I knew, with a deceptive smile, I would have done the same. Then we were off. The first thing I noticed were the cars. Hello there. The first one that was in the lane next to us was a Porsche 911 turbo in full body kit. Beautiful. Then there were Mercedes, Rolls Royces, Bentleys, and Ferraris. I kid you not, it was a wet dream. However, I was more of a bike guy and couldn't see any Harley-Davidsons which would have been the cherry on the cake.

The rest was a bit of a blur. We went through a tunnel and then we were on Hong Kong Island. It felt like I was watching a roll of postcards going past the window. Every view was amazing. My dad had gone to Hong Kong a few months before my mum and brother to get settled in and find somewhere for the family to live. His new company was paying for the flat, as was generally the case for expats. Accommodation, kids' school fees and even medical fees were covered.

We got out of the taxi and into this building on Conduit Road. It seems that my dad had found the most skanky flat he could. We walked down some stairs and into the flat. It was a dump. Built into the side of the mountain you walked straight into the main living area. The lounge and kitchen were combined. The kitchen must have measured four square feet and the lounge was dark and dingy. It had a window at the back that overlooked somebody's nice flat downstairs and their garden. We didn't have a garden.

There were two bedrooms and a disgusting toilet. My wee brother's room was filled with just a bed and a wardrobe. It also had a window that looked out onto what I can only describe as an open sewer from the top of the building to the bottom where water dripped continuously and which clearly contained some undiscovered microbes.

My mum and dads' room was just as bad. The whole place stank of damp. This was the high life, was it? From Newton Mearns, a nice suburb south of Glasgow, to this. I slept on the couch in the living room. My mum said that because I had joined the Navy, they didn't need another bedroom. What if I had ever wanted to visit?

After I had dropped my bags, I was full of energy, so we went out for my first real Chinese meal. It just wasn't the food that was amazing, it was the whole atmosphere. The waiter was friendly, chatting away in broken English. We tucked into the best Chinese feast I had ever had; every dish was completely different from what I had had before. The flavours, smells and textures filled my senses. At the end of the meal, I got my first-ever fortune cookie, 'Persevere and you achieve'. If you believed in omens, this one looked good.

We took a taxi home. I had a quick cigarette out the back door where I found more cockroaches than I thought existed on the whole planet. As they ran across my toes, I took a deep breath. 'Things are looking good', I thought to myself. And for a while they did.

第7章

After nine days in a withdrawal haze, I had suddenly become lucid. I woke in the morning with a whole bunch of emotions and thoughts that had not been possible whilst my brain was going through its readaptation to normality. I now found myself fully aware of my surroundings and situation and I now felt something new, a soul-crushing depression.

The feeling of total loneliness embraced me. Only my parents knew I was here. To everyone else in my life, it seemed that I had simply disappeared. It was as if I had fallen into a deep hole and no-one could hear me shouting for help. I desperately wanted to be able to connect with someone from my life, someone who knew me, someone I would feel connected to and who hopefully cared for me.

I could remember my dream from last night, the most lucid dream I'd had in months. Not lucid exactly but the first dream that was not filled with fear, dread, or self-hatred.

I dreamed of the year before I came to Hong Kong. I lay there in my prison hospital bed feeling finally rested and I had a dream about the time I used to think of as my worst years. The first weeks and months in Hong Kong had been the best in my life. But I did not dream of those times, I dreamt of the times before.

After breakfast, I approached the hospital orderly and, using my hands, made the internationally recognised gesture to write. I mimed writing and then outlined the shape of the paper to him hoping he would understand. He looked at me then looked around and gestured for me to wait. He left the cell when the guard opened the door and went off to start his daily duties.

So, I sat back down at the table where the others were preparing to start rolling out toilet paper and waited. Each prisoner was given four squares of toilet paper a day and it was our job to divide the toilet rolls into the four-piece rations that would be handed out in the evening.

At lunch, when he brought the bucket of congee and my piece of bread, cheese slice and cold milk tea, into the ward and put it next to the table, he silently gestured to me to come over to his bed. He bent down next to his locker, had a quick look around to make sure the coast was clear, opened it, reached in, and pulled out a notebook.

He looked over his shoulder and then quickly ripped out some pages and passed them to me whilst gesturing that I had to put them quickly into my shirt. Once I did that, he then found a pen and passed it to me, I quickly hid it and he nodded. He then made a gesture that I worked out that I had to give him the pen back, I quickly nodded again and then went straight back to the table with my hidden contraband. No one looked up from what they were doing, and I sat down and unwrapped my cheese and passed the disgusting tea to Danny the tranny.

There was a blank spot in the cell that when the cell door was closed and locked, the guards could not see. So that is where I decided to sit that afternoon. I did not know why I was forbidden to have the paper and pen but by the looks of everyone when I brought them out, I knew I had to keep them hidden from the guards.

I sat there and wrote in silence, the words flowing easily from memory to paper. He had given me ten pages out of his notebook, and I set out to fill every one of them with the story of mine and Gary's short but full friendship.

I filled those pages quickly, and easily. I could have written many more. I chose to write about Gary, Graeme and all the other friends from my last year in Scotland because my Hong Kong stories were still too raw, too recent and too painful.

I wrote all about the time we spent together and all the adventures we shared. For that short while of writing, and then reading it back, it took me out of there. I flew instantly back to those good times, times of pure joy. It was only then that I realised how special those times were.

When those visions slowly cleared, I found myself back to where my life choices had brought me. I was compelled to disclose, to declare, my deepest confessions.

I wasn't going to give up, deep in my subconscious, where my true essence lurked, hope also kept burning. Everything that had come before, what I had experienced, what I had done, survived, I genuinely thought that this was my fate, but another one I would get through.

My head swam with all these thoughts, trying to make sense of everything. I had nothing to plan towards other than going into the general population. I didn't know where I was in the process of justice. I had no idea what was going on or how long I would be held on remand. I had no idea what the future held for me, I just knew I had to survive day by day, learn as much as I could, and make my existence have some meaning.

Chapter Seven

I was up early with jet lag so, as was my routine after leaving the Navy, I completed ten sets of ten push-ups and one hundred sit-ups. I then sat at the dining room table and made myself a cup of tea whilst I considered what I was going to do that day. I knew what I wanted to do and I found it difficult not to just jump up and head out the door to explore the metropolis below me.

I looked around the tiny apartment, the whole place was smaller than our front two rooms back in Glasgow and the bad mouldy stink continued to linger. I'm sure there must have been better options. It looked like my dad went for the cheapest he could find, and he got it.

When my mum finally got out of bed, I could tell she wasn't up for much as she had drunk too much the night before, so I decided I would go out myself.

Ignoring my mum's comments and warnings but accepting the bit of paper on which she wrote our phone number in case I got lost, I exited the stinking, dark apartment and walked up the stairs to street level. I had been told that there was a little green minibus that would take me down to the city centre but I wasn't quite brave enough to try that out. So, as instructed by my brother, I turned right onto Conduit Road and walked along until I found the stairs where an old Chinese woman sold bananas.

It had all sounded completely surreal. I didn't know if I would even find any stairs and whether my younger brother was just kidding me, but there she was sitting or squatting more next to two large wicker baskets filled with bananas. She said something completely unintelligible to me and I smiled at her and looked past over her shoulder down some ancient-looking, wet slimy and broken stairs that led down and down and down at what was surely an angle made specifically for mountain goats, not humans.

I looked back at her, she couldn't possibly have brought those bananas up here, could she? My head would be full of conflict in the next few hours as that was how Hong Kong was going to introduce itself to me in innumerable ways.

There wasn't much of a view as I stood there. The space created by the steps was shadowed on all sides by tall old buildings, all with dripping air conditioners held at jaunty angles by rusting frames. The steps were slippery from humidity and little streams of dirty water seeped from the dilapidated walls that contained them.

The humidity allowed a natural biodiversity that I had never encountered before. Flaura and fauna survived between the concrete and the occasional mounds of garbage that had been there so long that they looked like part of the infrastructure.

There must have been 100 steps between Conduit Road and Robinson Road, where I now found myself.
Straight across the road was another set of stairs just as steep as the last. I followed these down and deeper into Hong Kong. Following my instincts, I wound my way through more and more streets, some not much more than alleyways. The buildings were so tall you couldn't tell the time of day. The noises and smells of a city waking up: cooking, shouting and lots of people clearing their throats.
Continuing my meander through pathways, streets and alleyways, I finally found myself staring down a wide section of stairs that seemed to slowly lead me through decades of history down to the incredible mega city below.

I stood at the top of these ancient steps staring at the first few floors of the highest buildings I'd ever seen.
Red taxis, blue double-decker buses, small cream and green minibuses and dozens of the most expensive cars available slowly merged like a modern dragon with multi-coloured scales. And people, people everywhere, thousands of them, following along the rivers of pavements.

At first, it was just a bobbling of black hair I could see, occasionally a dash of blonde or light brown would appear and disappear just as quickly. It was hot, my shirt was soaked to my skin, but they all seemed to carrying umbrellas to save them from a different kind of soaking. At the corner of one street, I could see an umbrella salesperson squatting next to their selection lying on a blue tarpaulin whilst they chatted to someone whose umbrella they were repairing.

It took some time to take it all in before I started to hear the noise above all the sound. It almost knocked me backwards when my senses finally accepted it. I carried on down the steps and entered the torrent of people. In amongst them, I noticed how smartly everyone was dressed and how smart the shops were that I passed. Gold shops with Chinese names, one with Rolex watches prominently displayed and with a man wearing a turban sitting outside on a stool holding what looked like an old shotgun.

I allowed myself to be swept along with the current of people until I found myself turning left onto Pedder Street. I had heard of this street as it was where my father's office was, World Wide Shipping was just two buildings down on the left side of the street. Just before that was the entrance to the Mass Transit Railway or MTR, Hong Kong's underground. More importantly for me, there was a small stall selling cigarettes.

Although I still had a few packets of 'Senior Service', the Royal Navy brand, I thought I would top up and find how much they cost here. The answer to that was nearly nothing, so incredibly cheap. I bought a few packets of Marlboro Red. I took one out and, whilst taking a drag, I looked around me, but mostly I looked up trying to take in the skyscrapers that seemed to bend in over me the higher they were. I carried on down towards where I believed the harbour was located.

At the next crossroads, my senses discovered something new, a 'ting ting' sound that I quickly discovered was coming from a couple of trams going in opposite directions. I crossed the road and found myself being directed up some stairs to an overpass. Still following everyone else, I moved towards another sound of a bell ringing, this one a bit more muffled. As we went round a corner, I found the location of the ringing. The crowd curved inwards away from the sound almost subconsciously, the sound of a bell hanging from a long stick wrapped in colourful tassels and being held by a man sitting on a mat of cardboard, dressed in rags and whose skin was covered in large boils and lesions. I had read a lot about it in many library books and had also seen pictures but here, unbelievably, right in front of me, was a leper.

Not wanting to stop and stare and naturally being carried forward by the crowd, I was quickly past him, but I found myself turning my head to look back at him. I felt caught between two different centuries, the modern and the old. I would see him many times in the coming months, taking time to see him when most others didn't.

I carried on thinking about him long after I passed him, so much so that I barely noticed that I was now walking down towards the Star Ferry Terminal and therefore towards the magnificent Hong Kong Harbour.

A three-dimensional, 360-degree science non-fiction movie is one way to describe what I was staring at from the harbour wall. Confused by the perspective of massive ships in the harbour dwarfed by the buildings on the other side and further away, I turned around slowly to try and find the depth and reality of space from the buildings and the hill behind me.

It made my brain dizzy. I staggered and realised that I was soaked to the skin with sweat. Clearly, I hadn't drunk enough water for my new home climate. I saw HMS Tamar and headed towards it remembering that's where I would get the small minibus back up to Conduit Road.

Over the next week, my mother and brother showed me around the place in more and more detail. We took the MTR, bus and even two different ferries to beaches, islands and even just the other side of the harbour. I soon learned that there was very little you couldn't do here within 30 minutes. It was a great first week that we spent together, and then my dad came back.

第8章

When I woke up, I had no idea how the day would play out. It was now two weeks that I had been in the hospital. It was a comfortable existence but with having so little to do, I could imagine slowly going insane in there. I'd seen my fair share of insanity during these fourteen days. There were three main types that I had the privilege to meet up close and personal. First was the Bambi, big staring looking eyes, mouth hanging open usually, possibly heavily sedated so they didn't say or do much. Then there was the chat show host. They would come flying into the ward as if on a stage, incredibly manic. That lasted a fleeting moment until they eventually started screaming and throwing things around. They became a bit more like Bambi as they were sedated before being removed and put into one of the single cells across from the main one.

Then there were the absolute psychos. They were never put into the big cell with us but always put straight into a single cell. They would talk to themselves or come to their door and stare into our cell, as if they were thinking, 'I'm so hungry, could I perhaps eat just a small part of each of you?' They were very scary as they could erupt without warning. I saw this tiny guy once having to be restrained by six guards as they tried to admit him to the hospital. He was frothing at the mouth as they tried to separate each arm and leg to try and control his thrashing. Another door was opened that I hadn't seen before and a guard fetched some sort of white padding. As they struggled to put it on him, I saw that it was a straitjacket. Wow an actual straitjacket, I didn't know they existed. The other door led into an actual padded cell. They eventually got him into it and shut the door. The noise stopped at once after the door closed, utter silence, it was weird.

After seeing the doctor, I was taken back to the hospital ward to collect the few belongings I had. This included the paper I had on which I had begun writing my diary again, along with the letter to Gary. I folded it quickly and put it down the sleeve of my white hospital shirt. I waited until the guard came to get me, followed his hand gestures to the hospital waiting room and sat down on the hard bench. There I sat and waited.

The hospital ward had always been warm. There was a thick pipe that ran around the walls, so hot that we could dry our shower towels on it and so hot that sometimes if you were not careful and brushed against it you could get burnt. The pipe did not follow into the waiting room so as I sat there, I slowly cooled down and started to feel the real temperature of where I was. All I was wearing was my thin white shirt and thin white trousers along with the rigid plastic sandals on my feet. No pants or socks so to try and retain what little warmth I had, I crossed my legs and crossed my arms to protect myself.

As I sat there, other prisoners came and went, all staring at me as if I were some sort of exotic animal. Lunch came and I was taken back to the ward to eat my bread and cheese slice. The tea was left to the other prisoners to enjoy along with their rice soup. Just as I was warming up, I was taken back to the waiting room at the front, at once feeling the cold wind coming through the bars of the glassless windows.

Sitting there shivering for a couple of hours, my thoughts took me back to that first night and the complete misery I had experienced in that cell. I tried to reconcile myself to the fact that I was ill back then, in the first stages of withdrawal, and even though I'd only been here for two weeks, I was a lot stronger but not quite back to my old self.

A guard came in and called my number,

'Yee chat sam say sam'.

I stood up and went towards the door. He pushed my shoulder towards the reception door next to the hospital. He said something but I understood nothing. I had started to notice the difference between the usage of words in separate places. I was used to the words used in the hospital; I did not know exactly what each syllable meant but understood the context of what I had to do when I heard each sound. I was never involved in conversations; it was always instructions. The hospital guards would give me different instructions from the other guards as they ordered me to do different things.

I entered the reception and the guard shouted something to the prisoner who worked there. He bent over, grabbed a blue plastic box and brought it over to me. Placing it on the floor in front of me, he turned and collected two more that were put side by side next to the first. Already shivering with the cold, I looked in each box which held different items of clothing. They smelt horrible.

One box had trousers, one was shirts and the third contained jumpers. I reached into the first one and was instantly grabbed, pulled back and told to get undressed first. It was still humiliating but not as embarrassing anymore. The wind was still flowing through the open door behind me, its icy wind puckering my nipples but shrinking my dick. The chance of taking my time to find the cleanest and least ripped trousers was now forgotten. No labels with small, medium or large, just a pile of blue cloth which I had to dive into, grab the first item and pull it on.

Skinny due to months of heroin addiction and minimal calorie intake, the waist size was not an issue. The trousers had buttons and string at the front to fasten. The ones I picked had two buttons missing, so I started to take them off when the guard stopped me with a shout. I tied them as quickly as possible whilst at the same time feeling the wind against my ankles as the trousers came halfway up my shins.

I grabbed a shirt from the next box, grimacing at the stink, and quickly put it on. It was so tight, it scraped across my skin. Had I not lost so much muscle, I would have ripped it by the slightest movement. Once again, it had less buttons than it should have, but I fastened what it had. I moved to the jumpers where the strongest stench was coming from. Eager to have one, knowing the warmth it would give me, but dreading it just the same. As my hand touched it, the coarse material almost hurt my fingers. Pulling it over my head felt like a thousand thorns being dragged through my hair and down my face. It was so tight it almost felt like a straitjacket, but it was warm.

Putting my sandals back on was not the easiest performance. My shirt and trousers were so tight they impeded my ability to move. I had the feeling that even trying to wish to complain to the manager may have been met with some animosity, so I completed the task as best I could. I had to leave the sandals unfastened because the lack of blood supply to my extremities was disabling. But at least I was warm.

The guard pushed me towards the door. With me came the stench that I would never become accustomed to. I could feel the cold against my legs and the tightness too.

He motioned me to follow him, so we started walking out of the area that had been my home for the last or, should it be, my first couple of weeks.

Although I would have preferred to keep my head down against the frigid wind that was swirling around the encased, grey surroundings, I wanted to look around as if for the first time. Those first couple of days were a real blur during the fever of withdrawal. I may have looked around but I did not properly take things in.

Now I recognised the dining hall to my right, filled with hundreds of prisoners wearing the same blue I was now in. We were walking through a caged walkway. Chain link fences on both sides with rolls of barbed wire at the top. On the left was a large brown mud area, only recognisable as a football pitch by the posts at either end. On the right, after the dining hall was a two-story area of buildings. I could not work out what they were.

Where they ended was another large building. But this looked different. It was surrounded by even heavier chained fences. There was what looked like a basketball court with a row of small cages running along its side. The building looked almost solid, like a fort, with only a small metal door visible on the outside. That was to my right. In front of me loomed three large buildings, not only dark like an old 1970s car park but a haunted one as well, very eerie. I recognised them from the first night and the first morning. These were the cell blocks.

I felt a shiver of fear and trepidation as we entered through the middle of the buildings. Climbing the stairs, I began to feel even colder than before, not only chilled to the bones but also chilled to the heart as well. Two other guards were on the first floor where we turned off the main stairwell.

After a brief interaction with my guard, he disappeared down the stairs and I was left with them. Number shouted at me, a quick gesticulation and I was led to the right and then directly to the left. We stopped at the very first cell. The guard opened the door, I stepped in and the door was locked behind me. The guard walked away and left me to be introduced to my new home.

Looking into the dark, once again lit only by a faint lightbulb, I began to take in my suite. On the left and at the back there was the low wall with what would be the hole on the ground behind it. Along the back wall from it was the sink and then right next to it, in the right corner, there was a small triangular plastic table with a small plastic stool. On the table was a yellow plastic mug. In front of the table and running along the right side of the cell was the plastic bed.

I reached my arms out to each side and could easily touch the both walls with flat palms. On top of the bed were some blankets which sat on a thin rattan mat. This was my bedding, a folded blanket, wrapped inside another one. The mat was my mattress. I took a step up to the blankets and ran my hand along them. If the fabric was just 10 per cent worse, it could have left tiny cuts in my hand.

I turned around to see the view from my apartment, hoping for the famous harbour view! I was pleased that this cell had a view out towards the other building with the basketball court. I could even see past it to the outer wall, the furthest uninterrupted view I'd had since I'd been here. I stood at the bars that ran the length of the front of the cell and looked out at the view.

My eyes were taking some time to focus. I tried blinking them, but I just could not get them to the level of vision

I'd had prior to being arrested and imprisoned. It worried me a little, but I put it down to not looking far for such a long time.

I turned back into my cell and decided to measure its length. Four steps and I was at the back wall. I tried the tap and, with much relief, found that I had free flowing water this time. I realised I was incredibly thirsty, so I took the mug and rinsed it out before I filled it and emptied the contents in one go. I tentatively turned to look at the toilet and was once again pleasantly surprised to find it clean. The whole cell was particularly clean with no dirt or dust or any faecal matter from the last occupant decorating the dull concrete walls.

Then I jumped, my heart started to pound, the adrenalin pulsed through me causing me to start to shake. I tried to compose myself because, in the distance, I could hear the scuffle of sandals coming from the direction of the stairs. Lots of sandals; lots of people. I stood there, like a shabbily attired statue representing a horror from the past that the sculptor had taken great pains for us not to forget. I was in the first cell on this corridor, I had no idea how many cells there were, but the corridor was long.

The next few moments could be important as it could form the basis of how I was viewed as a new member of the group. A group of people with whom I had no idea how long I would be mixed and no idea who they were. No idea what crimes they had committed and no idea of how they would take to me. I felt scared; I felt vulnerable. I knew that whatever happened in the next few seconds may well dictate the next few months. So, I went into fight mode.

I didn't want to show any weakness, but that had never been my strong point. I would stand up, I would face forward, prepared, not try to be invisible, to hide, but to be there standing right in front of them trying to show no fear by taking an aggressive stance. My screwed-up mind seeing this as my only way to survive. I wish I had decided to just be myself, but that self had long since gone into hiding.

The first faces turned the corner and stopped dead in front of me, 'Wahhh Gwai Gi, hi lee do ah' [foreign devil boy here]. The rest almost hysterically bumped into one another as they hadn't expected their daily walk back to their cells to be so inconveniently blockaded by the gawkers at the front.

I just stood there, putting on my strongest front whilst my behind trembled. Some of my new peers smiled as they were pushed past my cell, others just stared at me, then there were the others who just felt that they had to threaten me, try to scare me. I was hoping that the face I was wearing didn't show any fear but I feared that it did.

A shout from a guard and all the faces that had been leering at me suddenly snapped to the right and the last blue shirts and jumpers moved off down towards their cells. Doors were slammed and locked, a wave of clangs speeding away from me. Once the last had clanged shut, the thwack of the guard's soles echoed up the corridor. When he turned the corner, I finally sat down on my bed, exhausted from my Oscar winning performance.

As I sat there in my own silence, I listened to the new noise that filled the corridor of cells now complete with their human contents. There was a low hum of chatter, plastic tables and chairs being scraped across the concrete floors and the occasional threat directed towards my cell. I wasn't being completely paranoid as I could hear lots of 'Gwai Gi' and unless I was somehow confused, I was the only Gwai Gi in the area.

My body shivered, this time from the cold and I realised I was also hungry. Just as I was registering these two senses, a third and fourth kicked in. The sound of those big blue buckets being scraped along the ground and the smell of mountains of boiled rice that I could smell but would not taste. There was a feeling of joy and immediate deflation when I thought of what they were going to get to eat and what I was not.

As the first of the buckets rounded the corner in front of my cell, the prisoner in control of it stopped dead in his tracks. He stared at me whilst bent over his bucket, frozen until his partner bumped into him as he kept the momentum needed to direct the heavy bucket around the corner and along the concrete floor.

The knock shook him from his transfixion upon the strange white figure in front of him and he shouted 'Sik faan' [eat rice]. An officer just out of sight shouted something which I took to mean that the foreigner didn't get any as he at once started his bucket on its journey again leaving only the waft of freshly made rice, and whatever was in the bucket that followed, and not the taste.

There was another bucket, a yellow one. This was the tea bucket and once again it was moved swiftly past me to the next cell. I would have to wait for mine, I didn't know how long that wait would be, but my stomach told me that every second I had to wait was now a minute, and each minute was a minute too long.

It was still January and my hunger magnified the cold I felt from the wind coming through the open windows across from my cell. With no heating in the entire building, it would take days or even weeks for the concrete to warm up after the winter. I looked at my blankets at the end of my bed, placed on top of the thin reed mat and my heart sunk just a little bit more. The buckets had reached the end of the corridor, the continuous sound of their movement told me this as the noise crashed towards me, this time not stopping as it took the corner at high speed. I could smell the tea in the yellow bucket as it went past, it was warm and earthy smelling, I could taste it in my nose as I imagined sitting with a hot mug in my hands inhaling the scent as my hands acted as conduits to the rest of my body, directing the heat absorbed to the places that needed it the most. It was almost hypnotic what I was trying to do. I noted that I could really sense what I was manifesting, something I would come to rely on and strengthen over the next few years, years that I didn't know, I couldn't sense them, yet.

The corridor fell silent, each of the cells with their two occupants concentrated upon the hot meal that had been brought by the prison room service. I had not felt much hunger during the previous two weeks whilst I was withdrawing from heroin. My stomach had been dually constricted by the lack of food I had consumed what seemed like years ago on the outside and the nausea I felt during the time it took my brain to restart its own chemical systems after I had replaced them with the chemicals I had taken.

At least the pain was gone I thought as I sat there cold on my bed wondering when my food would come or even if they would bring me any. I looked up at the buzzer on the wall and the memories of the first night came back to me when no matter how many times I pressed, nobody came. So, what would be the point now of pressing it and asking politely if I was getting fed today? After two weeks I was already my own kind of institutionalised.

After all I was a nobody, a nobody amongst nobodies. I was already becoming aware of my place in the population's dynamic, and that was at the bottom. But I was a fighter, wasn't I? I had already made the choice to stand up for myself, I had made my mindset, I knew what it was like to be bullied.

At that point, I had a full body triple shiver. I shivered at the position I was putting myself into, I shivered due to the cold, and finally I shivered due to my hunger. I tried to think back to the hospital, to try and work out what time the food would normally arrive. I then tried to process the day that had just passed, the brightness outside, to see if the time just now was like the time before. No watches, no clocks, no routine, just existing. I knew I existed, but had they forgotten?

I was shaken from these thoughts by the overwhelming scent of oranges that suddenly filled the air. Oranges were my Achilles' heel in a way, they disgusted me. Fruit was a rarity in my house growing up, an orange perhaps showing up once a year around Christmas, never eaten, just there for decoration. Outside the home, when occasionally I had to eat one, all the reasons for my disgust would become clear: the skin sticking under your nail ripping it from your own skin; when the skin wouldn't come away without chunks of the fruit touching my fingers, the awful texture; the way that sometimes when you pressed through the skin, some of the juice would spray out of it leaving your hands sticky no matter how careful you were; and the most harrowing part, you never knew how it was going to taste.

It was like Russian roulette every single time. I hated them, I had another full body shiver just with the thought of them. However, now, all the things that I hated so much about them were juxtaposed with my desire to have one, no matter what the cost.

The scraping of buckets sounded again. They came round the corner with a shout that I couldn't understand and stopped at each cell to recover the now empty plates, but still I had no food. An officer stood at the top of the corridor, just outside my cell, I presume to ensure nothing untoward happened between the cells and the bucket boys.

He looked in at me as I sat there, arms wrapped around myself for heat. I looked at him for a moment and he said something to me whilst lifting one hand and two fingers to his mouth, making the shape of a question with his head and shoulders. I shook my head as an answer to what I thought was his question of whether I had eaten yet. He backed around the corner, and I heard him shout something about 'Gwai Gi and 'Chaan' [foreign food]. He came back around and gestured for me to wait.

It was starting to get dark outside when the footsteps returned. The corridor had been at its quietest after the others had eaten, the odd mumbled conversation stirred the stillness. I had helped myself to another cup of icy water from the tap and then used the hole in the ground to empty the little I had inside. At least I wasn't dehydrated. I then went to the bars and stared outside, trying to make out what I could. I saw some movement of prisoners back and forth, heard the shouts of the guards. I noticed their routine entering and exiting the gates that they needed to open and close to get to the other white building across from my building which housed the basketball court.

Focused on what was going on outside, I didn't register the sound coming towards me. A guard and a prisoner standing in front of me as if they had appeared from nowhere. In the prisoner's hands a yellow mug and a blue plate, the mug placed on the thin metal bar that ran horizontally and the blue plate put in the built-in slot between the bars that had been created for just this eventuality. It was two plates, one upside down on top of the other with a Post-it Note that had 'HOSP' written on it. Hospital. That's where my food had been taken to.

The top plate was removed and I was given a gesture to take both bits of plastic into my cell. I was not going to drink the tea, not only was it ice cold but it also had things floating in it such as rice and hair floating in it, apart from it being a rancid concoction of only slightly flavoured old sugary milk.

The à la carte dish contained 5 boiled potatoes that were an interesting colour and texture, an assortment of ends of vegetables that had been boiled and drizzled with an interesting gravy and a piece of a child's shoe, the sole from a leather one. This was made especially more fun and exciting now that my teeth had been weakened by my heroin addiction.

Of course, everything was cold, but I ate it like I was starving, which I suppose I was. I ate it with my fingers as I wasn't brought any cutlery. But I ate it, I ate every part of it, running my finger around the plate mopping up anything that remained. Then the buckets came back, three senses this time, the sound, the smell and finally a new one, heat. They stopped right outside with one bucket boy pushing two buckets.

'Chaa, lai?' [milk tea] he said to me as I sat there looking at him. I looked down at the buckets and saw that they were full of liquid, liquid I could smell and feel the heat. One was full of Chinese tea, an amber liquid with what looked like twigs and leaves floating in it, the other was full of hot milk, it was sweet hot milk, I could smell it. Each bucket had a mug floating in it. Instantly, I went to grab my yellow plastic mug and pass it to him. But just as I got to the bars, the guard shouted.

'Gwai Gi mo-ah! Gwai Gi on chaan' [foreign devil boy no, foreign devil boy foreign food].

With that the buckets were pushed away, along with their heat and sustenance. This wasn't the only evening snack as right then another prisoner came round the corner with a tray filled with bread, but once again the guard told him.

'Gwai Gi mo!' [foreign devil boy no] and his tray of bread followed him out of sight.

I was already still hungry after my dinner, but all of this just intensified my hunger. My daily food allowance was just not sustainable, it didn't take a genius to work that out. Two pieces of bread, two slices of cheese and what I just had for dinner constituted what they thought foreigners could survive on. Maybe I could if it also included a hated orange, hot tea or milk and some bread in the evening.

But as the radio came on with a local radio station playing canto pop, popular English music recorded by local bands and sung in Chinese and I was finally allowed to unroll my blankets and make my bed, I decided that I would try and work out how and who to ask if I could change to the Chinese diet, breakfast fish heads included.

On the hard bed I laid out the thin reed mat, it was falling to pieces, so I had to be careful not to have more on the concrete floor than my actual bed. I looked at the two blankets and tried to figure out how best to configure them. Comfort or warmth, those were my choices. I decided to start with comfort and then change to warmth if during the night it became particularly cold.

So, I laid one blanket on the reed, folding up the side that hung over the bed to try and create a kind of mattress and the other I laid on top, trying not to move them too much so that I wouldn't be engulfed in dust and whatever else lurked in them. There was also a small, hard, plastic pillow. About 3 inches thick and a foot long, just big enough for my head, and thick enough to keep me a wee bit off the bed.

I lay there for a while staring at the ceiling, trying to block out the noises surrounding me. I once again could hear people calling out to me, it was getting a little bit less intimidating now, but even so I was highly anxious for the days ahead.

When the first wave of sleep hit me, I pulled the blanket over me and closed my eyes. I would do this repeatedly every night, I didn't know how long for. I fell asleep.

Chapter Eight

After my experience of school in Scotland, school in Hong Kong was completely different and I was unprepared for it. My mum took me for a meeting with the principal at Island School. The school was mixed and had the Cambridge education system in place.

The principal was slightly concerned that I had missed so much school and the year had already started a couple of months prior to my arrival. It was looking as if I wasn't going to be allowed to join the school. But as I was sitting there, I analysed everything around me. This is something I have always had the ability to do. I see everything and I am able to add all this information together quickly.

So, just as my mum was about to get up and say, 'Thank you anyway,' I said that I was good at sports. I could play rugby, table tennis, cricket and chess and that I had done so at a high level in Scotland. It worked. I had worked out, by looking at all the trophies and medals, et cetera on the wall and remembering what I had read about these kinds of schools, that they were always interested in what they called 'jocks', athletes. The principal looked up and said 'Well, okay then. I think you can join the school!'

I was up early that first day. I had ironed my shirt and trousers the night before so only had to shower, shave, and have breakfast before I went up to the road to wait for the school bus with my brother. The shower was cold, but I barely noticed due to huge apprehension about my first day at school. I'd been through a lot in my short life so far, but it didn't stop the anxiety creeping up on me.

I decided to keep quiet and not talk. I would try to take everything in and not get engaged with anyone so as not to draw too much negative attention to myself. I was a lot stronger now having spent the last six months training in the Navy so I knew I could handle myself.

I had decided that no matter who the first person was that gave me trouble on my first day, I would hit first to let them know who I was and that I wouldn't put up with any shit. It was going to happen and I had to keep my wits about me. I wouldn't be at this school for long, only a year until I had finished my exams and left school finally to get a job. I could keep myself to myself for a year.

Keep my head down, do my work, make some friends but, most importantly, discover work opportunities in this amazing city. I didn't know exactly what I was going to do but it was a place where you could make money and a lot of it.

I waited for my brother and then we went out together. We climbed the stairs to the main entrance of our building and walked across the road to wait for the bus. We were the first there, standing outside number 7, Conduit Road. We were too early. It wasn't for another 10 minutes that the next school kid turned up.

From first form to fifth form you had to wear the school uniform but in sixth form you could wear whatever you wanted, within reason. I was never any good at clothes shopping and tended to choose the same things repeatedly. This time I looked as if I was still in the Navy. The clothes that I had bought had a remarkable resemblance to the number 8 uniform, blue shirt and blue trousers. Unfortunately, it was close to the school uniform as well. This was also causing my anxiety to increase.

My brother had told me about two bus prefects, older students who oversaw the overall behaviour on the bus.

One of them was all right, he said, but the other was a dickhead.

Eventually, the bus turned up at 0715. An old looking thing that said 'school bus' as soon as you looked at it. I didn't know what I was expecting, one of the green and white minibuses that did the route from HMS Tamar up here. But no, it was a full-sized bus.

We climbed on and I surveyed the scene. There were a couple of younger kids already on, staring out the window. Nobody took any notice of us. We went halfway towards the back of the bus and sat down. A younger kid sat in front of us and started talking to my brother who informed him that I was his brother and was starting school today.

It was a weird feeling. Here I was sitting on a school bus after being in the Navy for six months. I was carrying a school bag and not a Sterling sub-machine gun. Travelling in comfort and not in the back of a big truck with wooden benches, I'd seen pain and destruction and now I was staring at kids with bunches and rosy cheeks!!

However, it was still a scary experience. Just like the battle scenarios we had completed at basic training. All that training was going on inside my head as these 12-year-old kids were making pleasantries.

The bus stopped again and some older kids got on, still a year or so younger than me but I surveyed the threat and consciously prepared myself for combat. It was one of the bus prefects. He stared straight at me, came up to me and said,

'Who are you? You're not allowed on this bus!'

Confrontation immediately. I jumped up, spun him round, put his head into the crook of my left arm, grabbed the top of his hair, and smashed his face into the window across from me, sending younger kids screaming and diving out of the way as his whole body was sprawled across the seats.

Actually, that only happened in my head and whilst I was thinking about it, my brother said, 'He's, my brother. He starts school today and he's paid for the bus.'

'Well, I'm in charge of the bus'. He trailed away. I was just sitting there staring at him still thinking of how I would try to push his face through the window. He must have seen something in my face, so he just walked away and sat down.

Our apartment was halfway up the hill that was Hong Kong Island. The roads carved their way round it like a dragon's tail, all running parallel with each other as they snaked this way and that and joined each other at points due west or east so that the roads and homes sat on the side of the hill like terraces cut into the side.

This meant that the bus took a long time to get to the school as it wound through all these roads slowly filling up with a multitude of nationalities. It took about 45 minutes until it finally made the slow, gear-grinding trip up Bowen Road and then onto Borrett Road where it stopped at the back entrance to the school. Here, many more of the same types of bus, but all painted assorted colours, were depositing their cargo. There was also a school opposite ours filled with only Chinese students so there was a huge hubbub of noise and movement. However, I knew where I was going as I had been asked to report to the principal's office first thing.

My brother showed me how to get there from this back gate and I arrived just before the first morning bell went off. I sat there in that same waiting room that I had sat a few weeks earlier with my mum. I once again looked around at all the trophies and medals. I also took in a lot of the photos as well that dotted the wall with groups of smiling students and teachers and a smorgasbord of views and backdrops. I was kept waiting there for what seemed to be a long time, my anxiety rising all the time as I didn't know what was going to happen next. Another teacher passed me and went into the principal's office then I was called in.

As I walked into the office, the atmosphere was heavy, or was it just my imagination? Sitting behind his large desk was the principal and standing by his side was a teacher I hadn't met. He was quite an imposing figure. Tall, with a stern look. He had wavy dark brown hair and a beard. His eyes were locked on mine as if he was telling me, 'I'm in charge here'.

'This is Mr Harding'. I muttered a polite good morning to my new housemaster and then the principal began.

'Look, we know that you have been in the Navy and that worries us. You have also missed the first term of the year, so you are already behind in your class. We will not tolerate any bad behaviour or anything that causes disruption to this school. We will also not tolerate any reports of bad behaviour outside of the school, is this understood?'

'Yes', I said.

'Okay, then I wish you the best of luck. We have had a couple of new students recently that you will get to know, Melanie and Andy, and they have settled in well. We have also arranged for you to have a buddy who will show you around. If you have any problems, speak to them or see Mr Harding. Mr Harding will now take you to your first class.'

With that, I was dismissed. Mr Harding and I left the office together and went up a flight of stairs to the next floor where my class was and I was to be introduced to my new school buddy who would look after me.

Just after we had turned into the corridor to go to my class, the loveliest girl I had ever seen in my entire life came bouncing down the corridor with blonde hair flowing. I thought she was going to run past me and I was transfixed by this vision of beauty. But she stopped, right there in front of me. I had to check to see if my tongue was hanging out, my jaw was hanging loose.

'Hi, I'm Kylie'.

Those three words came to me as if they were separate. Separated by a period so that I could interpret what was happening to me right at that moment.

'Hi!'

She was talking to me. She was being friendly to me. This was something I had never experienced before. In my previous life, I had been mostly ignored, for the entire length of my life, people had never said 'hi' to me in that way before. It meant that she wanted to interact with me on a level that I had never experienced before. That singular 'hi' was the most incomprehensible 'hi' I had ever been part of, and the next word seemed to have been spiritually put there to amplify the first.

'I'm' ... she was introducing herself to me. She wanted to form a relationship of communication between us. She was also giving me her complete attention. Her body language was open and her eyes -- and my God what blue eyes -- were piercing like bullets into mine. I could almost feel the photoreceptors at the back of my brain starting to burn.

'Kylie'

Never has a name had such an impact on me. It summed her up perfectly. It was only just then when she uttered her poetic name that I was able to work out that she had an Australian accent. Every adolescent in the UK had been hypnotized by the antics of another Australian Kylie twice a day, once at lunch and once after Blue Peter, just before the 6 o'clock news.

As her alter ego Charlene Robinson, Kylie Minogue had blood running red hot for the last few years as she frolicked about in the paradise of Australia. And here I was standing in front of the most dazzling girl I had ever met, her bronzed, athletic body turned towards me. Her glimmering head of sunshine hair with her deep-sea eyes looking right into mine whispering romantic poetry into my ears and only for my ears.

'Hi. I'm Kylie.'

That moment was the most beautiful of my life and would be, well probably forever.

'I'm your buddy and I'm going to look after you'.

Had my entire existence up until that point been purposefully bad so that I would experience the joy of those few seconds at the highest level possible? Any higher and my heart may have burst right there and then. But it was just that and never anything else.

Having spent the previous years of my life searching for belonging, searching for love and affection, that moment I was experiencing was just that. There was nothing sexual about it at all. I didn't fancy Kylie; I never would, but that moment was still beautiful. It made me feel, well, perfect. I had always tried to mirror other people to try and fit in. I had done it so much that I now did it without thinking.

So, to mirror Kylie right there and then, that meant I was beautiful too, didn't it? Kylie took me to my class where I was introduced to everyone.

'Hi, I'm Derek, bet you don't know my nickname?'

'Eh, is it Del Boy?'

'What? How did you know?'

'Matthew. Everyone calls me Blakey'.

At the first breaktime, I had a huge group of people surround me all wanting to introduce themselves to me. It was intense. At my previous school, new kids were left by themselves, hiding in corners until they slowly made friends. In fact, that is what I had had to do for the last few years. But now I seemed to have a hundred kids all wanting to be my friend. To be honest, it was a little too much for me, I was overwhelmed.

During that melee of meeting new friends, I was invited to a birthday party that was happening that weekend. How I had longed to be invited to a party. I was usually a hanger-on, turning up to a party because one of my friends had been given an invite and they took me along.

Parties were so complicated to me. I stressed for a long time before going. Who did I want to be at the party? I had no real identity. I was always trying to be someone who others would enjoy being in their company. The clothes were a nightmare and I worried about how bad my acne would be. I tended to get drunk before any partying event. But I never stuck to any limits. It was the only thing that I knew how to do.

It gave me something to do when I was feeling uncomfortable. The problem was that I always drank too fast so was always having to get myself another top-up so that I wasn't standing still long enough for someone to try and engage me in conversation. How do you talk to people? What is the cool, polite, nice thing to say to someone who approaches you? I always felt such a twat on these occasions and my drinking habits helped me to become that twat quite quickly. Negative attention is what I got. I had been raised on it and I carried it on.

I had to be popular; there was no other way to be as a teenager. To become popular, I did things that made people laugh and therefore remember me. I got drunk, acted an arse, did risky things, and basically became the party fool. All I needed was the pointy hat and tights and I would have fitted the role of jester just perfectly.

So here I was surrounded by all these cool, foreign, gorgeous kids who wanted me to come to the party that weekend and they didn't even know me. This was an opportunity for me to reinvent myself. To become the cool person that everyone liked. Maybe even girls!

It wasn't even just a normal party; it was a boat party. I learnt that we would all meet up and head down to one of the piers at the harbour and go on Chinese junk that would head out into the sea towards some island somewhere. These junks are amazing vessels. I had seen that one when we were coming into land. This was going to be the best party I had ever gone to in my life.

When the bell sounded, I followed my class to the next lesson. I always stayed as close to Kylie as possible but with Blakey at my arm. I liked this guy; he reminded me a lot of myself. He was about the same height as me with blonde hair. He told me he was from Wales but had lived in Hong Kong for a long time. He had a kind smile and told me to stick with him and he would keep me right.

I scanned around the school on my way up to class. All the corridors were on the outside of the building, open to the weather. There were a few different buildings that were connected with open walkways and students were walking back and forward over them. There were open playing areas with lines painted on the ground for a multitude of different sports and next to them was a large area of steps whose purpose was really for everyone to be able to sit down and watch games that were taking place or chat whilst they were eating and drinking what they had got from one of the tuck-shops.

The tuck shops were just amazing. The chicken noodle soup would be the best I had ever tasted, and they also did polystyrene boxes of rice with pork and other delicious things. Blakey shouted at me to get moving, so I turned from my exploring to see him moving to a set of stairs towards our next class.

At lunchtime, Blakey took me to our house room. The students were split into different houses, I was in Rutherford. The older students all had their own common room, one for each of the houses: Da Vinci; Einstein; Fleming; Nansen; Rutherford and Wilberforce. They were a place for us to hang out during break or to 'study' during free periods.

On entering our common room, I noticed there was a bank of lockers on the left. Blakey told me to get a padlock and claim an empty one.

'I've got three lockers for all my crap,' he said, looking pleased with himself. The rest of the room was filled with chairs to lounge around in. There was a stereo playing music. Good music too, rock music. I was introduced to everyone in the room. Not everyone was enthusiastic about coming to meet me, but most were.

The rest of the day, I went from one class to another trying to see how much I would have to catch up with everyone else. Not much it would seem. Although I was three months late joining the class, I had a good background knowledge from all the reading I had done to understand what was being taught. In fact, I didn't need to do much remedial studying at all. I was up-to-date and even ahead of some in the class.

    I got to know more and more people. The person who I clicked with more than anyone else was the girl that I was told had also just started, Melanie. Tall, slim with strawberry-blonde curly hair that always smelled amazing, Melanie was drop-dead gorgeous. But she was also very grounded. She seemed to have effortlessly melted into the social structure at the school. The first time I met her was during a breaktime.

    'Hi I'm Melanie, do you smoke?'
    'Yeah'.
    'Come with us!'

    I followed her and a couple of others up a set of stairs that I hadn't seen yet. It took us up to part of the roof that led to the football nets that were stored up there.

    My God, what a view! Looking down from halfway up Hong Kong Island directly towards the harbour, I saw the postcard-perfect view that most people will know of Hong Kong. Looking down over the gleaming skyscrapers, it was an unbelievable sight over the harbour and the mainland beyond. The scene was shimmering in the late autumn heat with waves of mist caused by the humidity swirling around the peak of the island.

    I turned to see Melanie and a couple of lads sitting down leaning against a wall and pulling out their cigarettes. I accepted a Marlboro Red from Melanie and sat down with her. One of the other lads was Andy, who had also just started school. Both were from England and even a blind man could see the flirting going on between them. If they weren't going out already, they certainly sure would be soon.

It was an exotic experience sitting up there just below the roof overlooking the harbour ... almost romantic.

'Are you going to the boat party this weekend?'

'Sure. It sounds amazing.'

'We usually go to Thingummy's on a Friday night then there is the beer buffet at the In Place later. Do you fancy coming? We all go every week.'

'We meet at the corner of Pedder Street. Do you know it? Anyway, we meet next to the ATMs and then all head over to the In Place together, some go to Thingummy's first. You wanna come?'

'Absolutely.'

We finished our cigarettes and headed back downstairs. After that first roof experience, I could generally be found there at regular intervals during the day.

At the end of the school day, I met up with my brother.

'I'll show you where the school bus is', he offered.

'No, it's ok. I'm heading into town with some of the others.'

I met up with a group that were heading down into the town. Across the road was a path that wound through the woods towards the other paths that lead down through all the winding main roads, eventually arriving in Central.

A load of kids stood next to a long wall at the top of the path talking, some smoking. I joined the group of smokers and was introduced to kids I hadn't met yet. I felt like the centre of attention and it felt great. The girls looked fine in their own clothes, being sixth formers. The climate was a tremendous help as most had loose-fitting clothing over their tanned, healthy bodies. Pretty, pretty, pretty, all of them, and they were all talking to me. I didn't know where to look.

After a cigarette, we started to walk down through a series of lanes and paths through the bewildering array of buildings, down through the humidity and towards the bustling metropolis below us.

Before I knew it, we were walking into McDonald's. This would be a treat. But McDonald's was not cheap, I remembered. In Scotland, it was a few pounds for a meal. I didn't have enough money with me to buy anything, so I didn't know what to do. I didn't want to have someone buying for me so when I got to the service counter and looked at the prices, to find the cheapest item.

I was staggered to see that I could afford everything. A Big Mac was only about 20p. I bought two and went to sit down with my huge group of new friends. I sat back and ate whilst listening and watching. This was amazing, I was part of this dynamic straight away. No one was giving me a tough time. No comments were thrown towards the new guy. The feeling of acceptance filled me. I was overflowing with happiness.

Back home that night, I lay down on my bed -- the sofa -- and tried to take it all in: the weather; the location; my new friends; the girls. It was like the perfect dream, but it was reality. Had all my previous worries built me up to this wonderland of love and friendship, opportunity and my future?

I decided to write a letter to my couple of friends back in Scotland. Maybe I was gloating, I don't know, but I wanted to tell them all. Maybe even to say to them that there is a brighter world out there, Glasgow was just a pit of despair and that the rest of the world was different.

第九章

The reed mat was on the floor and both hairy blankets were wrapped around me, my feet freezing lumps hanging out the end. I had my full uniform on apart from the rigid plastic sandals, without socks. My shoulders and hips felt bruised from their night of tossing and turning on the solid surface trying to find the most comfortable uncomfortable position. Once I had managed to wrap myself, any movement had to be tiny so as not to undo my cocoon and let any warm air out and cold breezes in. It was still only the middle of January. There were three types of shivering that morning in the semi-dark before the lights and radio came on: hunger; cold and fear.

I lay there for as long as I could. A guard walked past my cell and down the corridor to do the thing they did every 30 minutes throughout the night that made a tapping noise, usually three times. I had heard the same in the hospital, but it echoed loudly here. I closed my eyes again as he passed my cell on his return, childishly closing my eyes thinking that if I couldn't see him then he couldn't see me.

I was becoming increasingly terrified about the day ahead as I knew I would be leaving the cell and mixing with the rest of the remand prisoners.

Suddenly the cell was in full light and the radio crackled to life with the shouting in Chinese. I still have no idea of their meaning or what they were ordering me to do. But I knew that it was the signal to get out of bed.

Within a minute another guard was outside, baton outstretched and banging each bar of every cell as he walked down the corridor shouting something that was becoming familiar.

'Hai sun', get up, I had deduced.

I swung my feet off the bed, and onto the floor and quickly jerked them back up from the icy cold concrete. I found the discarded reed matt and placed it next to my bed so I could finally stand up and stretch out my aching bones.

My eyes were red and caked in dirt from the blankets, so I shuffled the matt over to the sink and pressed the metal tap for water. It came out in a slow dribble. It took me a moment to adjust my hands so that I could cup some of it and raise it to my face to wash the grime away.

I had to take a deep breath and compose myself for the cold. I cupped handful after handful to throw over my face and then bravely put some over my head to wash my hair. Well, wet it at least.

My body was skin and bones, but my hair was thick and long. I could feel the knots in it from my disturbed sleep. I fetched my mug and took a couple of mouthfuls of water before I turned to my bed to fold the blankets.

I tried to remember how they looked so that I could reproduce the pile that I had found the night before. Eventually, after a few attempts I had created a lopsided version of what I had found. With the pillow placed on top, they looked as bad as I felt. I had a pee and then sat back down on my bed, legs and arms crossed trying to keep any warmth I had from the blanket workout.

Adrenaline is an amazing thing and, probably without me knowing, it was the only thing that was keeping me going. The stress I was under was keeping the hunger at bay, for now, but it was making all my senses extra sharp. I was jumping at any noise, waiting for that final moment when the guard came to unlock my cell door and force me out into the corridor to finally face the others.

I was frightened and, because I was finally free from withdrawal symptoms and the last remaining traces of heroin in my brain, I was lucid enough for this to be the most frightened I had been so far. It was super sharp compared to the blurred fear of the past two weeks.

I wasn't only frightened of who the other prisoners were and what may happen to me but also because I had no idea what the process would be for the day ahead ... the days ahead.

We were the first corridor to be unlocked. I could hear the others being freed from their overnight capture. The clatter of doors, the shouting of guards, but no noise from the prisoners. Silence was strictly enforced and noise was not allowed.

There was a hushed whisper from my corridor before the guard came round the corner and shouted something down the corridor before turning to my cell and unlocking my door. It swung open, an invisible force drew me towards it and I stepped out, the rotten and thick air from my cell almost pushing me out like the bubbles from a bottle.

As I was the first out and I didn't know the rules, I just stood there outside my cell. I looked down and started to meet my new housemates. I was very scared. I had been scared all night thinking about this moment. The two weeks in hospital had introduced me to the brutality of life in Pik Uk.

The daily admissions of the bloodied and wounded which always followed the sounding of the alarm and the thumping of the guards' boots as they ran excitedly towards the scene. Then came the beatings and the screaming and the opening and shutting of a single cell into which the unfortunate prisoner was thrown by the laughing guards.

I tried to compose myself but any of that was shaken out of me when the guard came back up the corridor and burst my thought bubble by shoving me and shouting at me to move forward. I walked round the corner where I found two other guards standing in a small office area.

One shouted at me and the other pushed me against the wall, shouting sounds that had no meaning to me apart from the ubiquitous fuck you, foreign devil. I stood there as the rest of the prisoners filed past me. I felt that I was suffering the triad fate of death from thousands of flying daggers, judging by the looks I was getting.

Some of the prisoners, many covered in tattoos, were angry and some I knew were just trying to intimidate me. I knew that because it was working. As the last prisoner passed me, I was pushed into line behind them. I followed down the stairs until I was standing at the back of two lines formed automatically by the more experienced inmates.

Here, I began to see the hierarchy. The bigger and more tattooed the inmates were at the front and they all seemed to have the best clothing including jumpers and jackets!! Their hair also seemed to glisten in the morning sun and some had a comb stuck in their quaffed and slick hair.

They all carried blue bags that appeared ready to burst, filled with I had no idea what. Some of them looked like they were off for a lovely day at the office and some looked like they were off to the gas chamber, me included.

As soon as I joined the back of the line, an order was called out and the line started to shuffle forward. The shadow of the buildings still made me shiver. I could see where the sunlight finally reached the earth in front of me and so I focused my senses on soaking up as much as I could to try and warm my bones. Unfortunately, when I finally stepped into the sunbeam, I also stepped out of the protection the buildings were giving from the wind, so any warmth to be had was just as swiftly blown away.

There was no talking, just a couple of hushed whispers here and there, until we eventually arrived at the side entrance of the now-familiar dining hall. The first guard took his keys out and used them to knock on the door. A thin plate slid open, not unlike what you'd see at a speakeasy in Chicago during prohibition, a guard looked out and slid the plate shut and almost instantly the door opened.

This had to be a regimented routine, something the guards had to do rather than what was necessary as it had to be the exact same routine every single day, at this near exact time. With that thought came my very first, lucid moment when I considered planning how to escape.

Have you ever stood outside a restaurant, absolutely starving, knowing that you're about to get a free meal, but feeling no joy at the thought? Even at the back of the queue, I could smell the food, I could feel the heat from the kitchen. I stood there, shivering, with a wave of depression sweeping over me, almost in tears knowing the hunger and cold that awaited me for at least the next seven hours ... seven days ... seven weeks ... seven months ... each one felt like seven lifetimes.

Each inmate walked up to a large metal shutter and a blue plate heaped with rice, some veg and a couple of fish heads or tails was pushed under the shutter for them along with a yellow mug of steaming hot black tea. They then grabbed chopsticks and a plastic spoon from two basins before they turned and followed a pre-set path towards one of the metal tables that filled the hall. As the last of them gathered their breakfasts, I stood there waiting for a guard to bang the shutter with his baton and shout

'On Chaan'.

Then there would be a pause. I stood there waiting, watching the others dive into their huge plates. Filling and warming their bellies, you could feel the heat of the room increasing. For them, the heat was from the inside out. For me, it would be only the outside, never quite warming my insides.

A few minutes passed and eventually a blue plate was pushed out. There it was, a piece of bread and a cheese slice. With growing despair, I gathered my food and waited for the yellow mug to follow. Perhaps it was just my imagination but I swear I could hear voices from behind the shutter laughing as the mug with hot, sweet, milky tea was pushed out.

The tea probably had more protein and vitamins in it than the food. But it wasn't the ones you would happily digest, they were all of human origin and floating on the top in a vulgar display. I had to pick the mug up, even though it was so repulsive, and I walked to the last table where others had now finished half of their meal.

I had nearly sat down with the last few prisoners when a guard came over, grabbed my arm, pointed his baton to an empty table and shouted.

'On Chaan'

I was being forced to sit apart from the others, perhaps to stop me from eating their food but probably to stop them from eating mine or maybe simply for my own safety. That thought did not make me feel any safer.

So, I sat where I was told, facing towards the others and was at once thrown back to primary school when I was forced to sit at another table in the classroom because a psychologist had told them to separate me from the others due to my heightened intelligence!

It was then that my shaking interrupted my thoughts, hijacking me once again along another rail track of psychological torture. I had been shaking from the very moment I woke up this morning. I had been under incredible levels of constant stress for weeks. How much adrenaline does the human body have the ability to create? I was shaking because I was cold, I was shaking because I was scared and I was shaking because I was starving. Now I was shaking because I realised I was shaking.

Pushing the mug of human excreta disguised as tea as far away from me as possible, fully aware of the hundreds of eyes staring at me, I picked up my cheese slice, unwrapped it and placed it on my piece of slightly stale bread, making sure there was an equal gap from the edge of the cheese all the way round from the edge of the bread.

I measured down one side and then the opposite side and pushed a small indentation into the crust, thus when I folded the bread over, I had created a perfect sandwich. Once folded I carefully pushed the bread down making it more compact and therefore, I thought, tastier.

I was going to take my time; each bite would be savoured, and the mastication extended for as long as possible as I had read somewhere that the more you chew the more you fool your brain into believing that you are eating a large meal. I think it was during my six months in the Royal Navy when we were on a survival exercise on Dartmoor that I learned that.

With a sudden eruption of noise from the back of the dining hall, I realised that although I had all the time in the world, that time wasn't mine. The first table had stood up and was now walking towards the front of the dining hall. I now looked to see the side door open with a guard standing there. Breakfast had finished before I had taken my first bite.

Already wanting to become meddlesome and regain some form of control, I slowly took my first bite. I looked at the remaining sandwich and tried to calculate how many bites I could take from it whilst I began counting my chews, twenty-one was what I was aiming for each bite.

The tables were standing and clearing at regular intervals. Not only did I quickly realise that I didn't have time for the remaining bites to be chewed twenty-one times, but I also didn't know if my jaw muscles would have the energy. With a slight feeling of defeat, I consumed the rest of the sandwich with fewer chews and bites.

I had tried to take some control of my surroundings but had failed. I felt it in my soul. It might sound like a tiny thing of literally zero importance but, for me, any small amount of success from this point forward would help my ability to survive the situation that I found myself in.

I was completely unaware of the time but I knew that my stomach was still empty with another three or four hours until lunch. I was still cold so any energy that the sandwich had given me would be quickly used up trying to heat my core whilst my extremities would remain frozen.

When I was told to get up from my seat and move to the door, I had to hold onto my thin blue trousers to stop them from falling. At the door, the cold January air wrapped its calorie-hungry arms around me.

Behind me, the door from the kitchen opened and four or five prisoners came out to collect the big buckets in the middle of each table into which diners place their used plates and cutlery. With dirty rags in hand, they quickly gathered and wiped at the same time almost in a silent ballet moving to set choreography.

When I looked around, all the other prisoners were standing staring back at me lined up just as we were when we arrived. I was ushered to the back of the line, trying to ignore the stares and the whispered, what I took as threats, words directed towards me. The hate in some of their eyes was something that I had never experienced before. I wasn't a stranger to people not liking me, but this was different. Some of the looks poured out the purest of hatred.

I hadn't got to the back of the line when it had already started moving forward, back into the dining hall. I was still having to hold up my trousers so they wouldn't fall to my ankles. I noticed a few of the others doing the same and others in what looked like new clothing, all nice and warm compared to my ice-cold feet and shivering torso.

Everyone took to their tables again, six at each. I was stopped at the door as the others all started to sit down. There was a quick chat between the guards which resulted in me being put at a table by myself once again.

Apart from the clean tables, there was also something else different. On one of the tables at the front of the hall, there were now old, torn, tatty boxes. Once we were all seated, one table at a time, one prisoner from each table was told to go to the table with the boxes. Out of each of the boxes were taken what looked like boards, books, newspapers and magazines. This was the entertainment for the day.

I sat there watching and waiting. When every table had finally got what they wanted, I was told to go and get something for myself. I walked to the table and investigated each box. The first one was boards with geometrical designs on one side and small sliding lid boxes.

I slid one open to find small round wooden discs with a Chinese character on each. Chinese Chess? Didn't know it, couldn't play it and didn't have anyone to play with so I moved to the next box which had several small paperback books, all Chinese obviously, and some old newspapers and magazines, also all in Chinese.

I shrugged my shoulders and just turned and went back to my seat. Taking anything, I thought, would have been a pointless exercise. I sat back down at my solitary table and just watched as the others' time passed faster than mine.

The dining hall was cold, with wind from the barred windows whipping around or from under the steel access door. I saw that the others all huddled together whilst playing chess or reading. All I had were my arms to try and keep me warm, the cheese and bread not creating very much thermogenesis in my stomach. If I thought of a body part, I instantly felt that it was cold. Sitting on the bare wooden bench, my emaciated arse offered little padding.

I looked at the shiny metal top of the table in front of me. I leant forward, crossing my arms as I laid them on the table, thinking that I could lay my head down upon them whilst I daydreamed myself out beyond the walls that surrounded me.

BANG!

'Hai sun!'

Obviously lying down wasn't going to be a possibility.

I sat there, eyes down, not ready to make eye contact with anyone, not just yet. I had other senses tuned into my surroundings, keeping me safe whilst I tried to think of a story from the past to think about to pass the time.

Weirdly, it wasn't long until lunch was called. They had their white or green congee and I had my slice of bread and cheese, oh and the disgusting tea. The tea was ignored, I made my sandwich, ate it, took my plate and mug to the big shutters as instructed, and returned to my table.

Just as I sat down, a guard shouted something and immediately a lot of prisoners got up and went to the lectern, put something onto it and went back to their tables. No one told me what was going on. I never asked anyone what was going on. I spoke to myself; the only words now were inside my head.

Sometime later the same guard shouted something again and all those who had got up earlier got up again and went and lined up at a new door I hadn't seen before, just to the right of the kitchen shutters. They lined up in a single line but this time they all had what looked like a small face in their hands. I realised what it was. They were lining up to go for a shower. A washcloth or even soap was something I didn't possess.

When I turned back from staring at the line, I noticed one of the guards looking at me. Our eyes came together for a second or two before he looked away and I just went back to my thoughts again. I heard the door opening behind me and everyone going out. They came back ten or fifteen minutes later; I could smell them before I saw them.

THINGUMMYs

Chapter Nine

So here I was, 16 years old and getting ready to meet my friends to go to a club, not an under-18 disco, but a proper club. Looking in the mirror, I smiled to myself. I put my best clothes on and headed out. The night was dark and I was leaving too early, but I couldn't help it. I was going to walk down to Central for the first time at night by myself.

I decided to go via 'crunch alley' at the back of our apartment. A dark alley so filled with cockroaches; every step was met with a satisfying crunch of half a dozen of their bodies. It led down a dizzyingly steep set of stone steps, most broken and cracked down into the darkness at the back of the poorly named Emerald Court, flat 2B, or not 2B, of 14 Conduit Road, towards Robinson Road which ran parallel but a good hundred feet further down the side of the island.

I walked through another dark alley, across a road to yet another dark alley until I came out onto the busy streets of Central District. I wandered through the high-rise buildings, one out of thousands, heading towards my destination. I already knew Pedder Street well, past the cigarette seller and one of the many entrances to the MTR. Right at the top of the street were a couple of ATMs belonging to the Hong Kong and Shanghai Banking Corporation. Right next to them was a low ledge. I hopped up on it and waited for my friends to arrive.

Pedder Street acted as a funnel for the slow-flowing traffic trying to get from the higher part of the island to the lower part where people caught ferries or buses to the rest of the colony. The flow was nonstop with red taxis, buses and luxury cars all fighting for their own piece of tarmac.

On each side of the road were people all seemingly travelling in the same direction. With the MTR and the Landmark shopping mall on the other side of the road, the pavement was always busy. I sat there almost invisible to it all, able to melt into the background without anyone paying me any attention.

As I was early, it was a good thirty minutes before others from school started to arrive. Everyone was dressed to impress. There was an even mixture of guys and girls, and I have to say that all the girls looked gorgeous.

So, was this a normal Friday night in Hong Kong I wondered to myself. As we waited and chatted, people came up to introduce themselves to me. I thought of my past and realised that I was only really appreciating what was happening now because my life back then was so shit. But I would keep that to myself. At the allotted time, we all headed towards the nearest MTR station and bought our tickets to go to Tsim Tsa Tsui. The last MTR was around 1 o'clock, so that was when we would be coming back.

We all jumped on the first train that came into the station. We practically filled the carriage. Some were already drunk, having started drinking earlier and were dancing and singing in the carriage. Some of the local Chinese were clearly disgusted by our behaviour and moved as far as possible away from us. I just sat there smiling and talking to some of my new friends.

Arriving in Tsim Tsa Tsui, we all piled out and danced and sang all the way up to the street. The Inn Place was just off Nathan Road on Hangkow Road. When we got there, I could hear the music coming up a set of stairs where a big neon sign signalled our arrival. At the bottom of the stairs, the beat of the music filled all my senses with excitement.

There was a big, burly English guy sitting at the bottom of the stairs and we handed over our HK$50, about £4, and he either gave us a voucher for two drinks or a stamp on the back of the hand for the beer buffet.

I took the stamp and walked up to the bar with the gang, showed my stamp and the young Chinese guy behind the bar filled a pint glass with San Miguel. We were away. I had to keep hold of the pint glass as it was a buffet. I could go up to the bar and have it filled as many times as I wanted to, all night! Mentally looking around, I could tell there was absolutely no one over the age of 18.

It had the look and feel of an under-18 disco, but it was a nightclub with all-you-can-drink beer. So, we drank, we danced, we laughed, and we got drunk, inebriated to the point of having to go to the toilets and throw up.

I got to know the staff behind the bar quickly. The guy who kept serving me was called Ricky and the gorgeous waitress who was hanging around in her white shirt and short black skirt that framed her amazing body was called Eddy. I spent a lot of time talking to Eddy; she was just fabulous. She may have been five years older than me, but we hit it off quickly. Towards the end of the night, I found myself staggering over to a seat and looking around.

'Whatever you do,' I thought to myself, 'Don't fuck this up. You're in heaven, buddy'.

'Last MTR' went the shout. It was a call for the gang to get together and stagger up the stairs quickly to catch the last train. If we missed it, we would have to pay for a taxi to get back over to the island through the tunnel.

I had been told that the taxis didn't like crossing the harbour at this time of night and would charge double. How we made it up the stairs, let alone to the MTR station, I have no idea.

Everyone was pissed. I mean really pissed. There were kids puking in doorways, others latched onto each other, with faces that may never be pulled apart. Hands down trousers, with penises sticking out, hands up skirts with hands frantically looking for buried treasure. It couldn't just be a normal Friday night, could it?

And to think that tomorrow night was an actual party, a birthday party on a Chinese junk. I was too drunk to feel overwhelmed. I just followed the crowd to the station, stepping over vomit. When we got on the train the pissing, vomiting and mutual masturbation didn't stop. It was like an orgy. My head was rolling about, trying to see through unfocused eyes, and now we were off to a place called Thingummy's.

Walking towards the small roads that start at the bottom of the island and end up at the Peak, I stared at all the neon signs declaring the finest accoutrements the modern man and women needed: Rolex watches, Benetton clothes, for example. Signs for restaurants, bars, and others in Chinese with bright yellow backgrounds. This was the high-end shopping district of Hong Kong. It was like walking through a modern cavern with buildings seemingly leaning over us as if they were touching; they were at such a great height.

We walked up to a long street on the right and followed its shop windows, some with fish tank walls with a restaurant hidden behind where its patrons could choose the freshest of fish. The area started to become a little bit grubbier. The side street was a street that I was more used to, a bit greyer, like Glasgow.

At one point, all the unfamiliar odours gave way to something that was all too familiar -- the smell of urine. Yuck, I thought someone had been using one of the many tiny narrow alleys that ran off the street as a toilet. I would be wrong to think that. The stink was coming from an open doorway, and above that doorway was a sign that welcomed us to Thingummy's. Through my drunken haze, even I could recognize a shithole when I hadn't even seen one yet. But looking around at the well-dressed and somewhat naïve fellow students, I had to trust my gut. If this was Glasgow, there would have been no way I would have entered such premises. In Glasgow, these places only meant one thing: drunken violence; sectarian singing, and more drunken violence.

As I entered the dark hallway, I became aware of something sticky on the ground immediately under my feet, the carpet. I walked forward and, in the gloom, I could see the top of a staircase that curved downwards to my left.

'POW'.

The hit came from the right-hand side, I had been too slow to respond. I had been stupid, I thought. It was a trap. The hit knocked me into the wall to my left, and plaster flew everywhere. I gagged as I realized that it wasn't a hit made of matter; it was pure gas. I strained through my tear-stained eyes, trying to rub the stench off them, and could just make out two toilet cubicles, wood rotten, doors hanging off.

'Don't go in there, mate', one of my new friends uselessly informed me.

As I managed to crawl past the crossfire of putrid stench, I reached the top of the stairs. It was only then that the noise from downstairs could permeate through the stench. Like chemical warfare, the two senses fought for prominence, and now sound won.

As I walked down the spiral staircase, the hum of voices joined in with the music. I was descending into some sort of Dickensian fairy-tale, a bar filled with only teenagers. No, not a bar, a cave ... not a cavern, but a cave. I passed an old black telephone on a small shelf and surveyed the scene below me.

To the left was a curved bar where an old Chinese guy stood in front of various drinks on the optic. There were adults in here as well ... there were three sitting at the bar. But the rest of the view was filled with teenagers all sitting around on old seats with no discernible colour.

Each group was in small alcoves, curved cushioned seats with tables. There were also seats lining the walls of what looked like panelled wood but they were difficult to make out with the explosion of a multitude of graffiti marks left by visitors over the years. It looked like it had been over hundreds of years.

In one corner was an old jukebox that was responsible for the music that filled the small space almost as thickly as the fog of smoke that had been expelled by these teenagers. It was, in anyone's eyes, a dump, but it was a dump where smartly dressed kids could come and fulfil their desires which I could only guess not only included alcohol.

We all got pints of San Miguel and squeezed into spaces that others made for us. I spent the rest of the night trying to read the graffiti, meeting new people, and settling into, although I didn't know it, what was going to be my home for the next few months. I was happy, drunk and comfortable. I had a family of friends around me like I had never had before. These were my new family. Away from the real family that I had felt I had never been able to fit into. I felt safe and loved for perhaps the first time in my life. This is where I wanted to be.

第10章

On this, the second day, I felt less on edge. Knowing the routine was a big part of that. It was the morning and we had just completed the get up, move outside, move back inside routine and I headed straight to what was now my designated table. I even had a plan for the day ahead.

As I had enjoyed my daydreaming so much the day before, this time I didn't even bother looking at the boxes of entertainment. I just sat at my solitary table and carried on from where I had left my thoughts yesterday.

Although talking was not allowed, there was some whispering going on that the guards ignored. The guards stood next to a lectern at the side of the hall. One would regularly take off on a walk around the hall occasionally stopping at a table to watch a game of chess. Most of the guards smoked, sometimes going right up to prisoners and dangling their cigarettes in front of them. When they had finished, they stood the cigarette upright on a table at the front of the hall so that it would burn all the way down leaving no chance to get your hands on a butt to smuggle back to your cell.

However, I'm sure that some of the prisoners got their hands on some from certain guards. As Lennon, my Triad boss. repeatedly told me.

'Police Triad. Courts Triad. Prison Triad' meaning the Triad had infiltrated the very top of society. That meant that some of the guards were Triads. I looked around the hall and tried to work out if any of our guards had a secret.

I knew some of the different Triad gangs: 14K; Sun Yee On; and Wo Shing Wo, which was the Triad gang that I hung out with, may have had guards as members, but even if I knew, I could never tell anyone, never. I knew the rules.

Lennon shared many things with me about the Triads, but I wasn't ever one of them. I knew there were lots of distinct levels in the gangs and that each member had to do what anyone above them said. If they didn't, it meant the one above 'lost face' so had to punish the one below. I'd seen Lennon do that, it was always instant and violent. Not as violent as when two different gangs had fought together. I'd seen that once, meat cleavers and short baseball bats, not easy to forget.

The triads were part of the hierarchy in the prison. The top guys were the local Hong Kong Chinese; they ran the place. They had a top dog in each cell block and dining room. He had his second in charge and everyone fitted into their gang at various levels.

Then there were the mainland Chinese, the IIs [illegal immigrants]. They also had their hierarchy but theirs was more makeshift. It was always changing because they tended not to stay on remand for long, receiving six-month sentences fairly swiftly.

Then there were the Vietnamese guys, or Vietnamese dogs as they were called. These guys were the most dangerous of all as they had nothing to lose. They had either escaped Vietnam on a boat with their whole family only to be put into a detention centre or were born in the detention centre. So, when they were released from this prison, they went back to the detention centre. They did not care. Some of them had already lost their whole family when their boat sank.

I met one guy who had watched his whole family drown, one by one, before he was 'rescued' and thrown into a detention centre. I visited one of these centres a few times when I was at school to play table tennis and instruct the kids about computers as a volunteer. Depressing places; yes, even more depressing than this place.

Later that second morning, we were told to get up and we were moved outside only to line up once again. It was lunchtime. We went back in and collected our lunch. I went to my separate table and sat down.

I was about to start eating when there was a huge crash. Two of the Vietnamese dogs had jumped on top of another guy. They had chopsticks in their hands and they were stabbing him ferociously in the back and the neck. It happened so quickly; the guy had no chance, they attacked him from behind.

Just as quickly, an alarm went off and all the guards started running towards the fight. They grabbed the two perpetrators and started beating them up. Very quickly, we were told to get up and leave the hall. I turned back to see the other guy still sprawled out over the metal table with blood slowly covering it and dripping off the edge.

I never found out what happened to the guy. I did not know what would happen to me.

Chapter Ten

It was Saturday morning, the day of the boat party. Feeling a bit rough from the night before, I had to get up to head into the town and get a haircut. My first thought on waking up was:

'What am I going to wear?'

So, I met up with Matthew Blakey who had offered to show me where to go shopping.

My wardrobe was not pretty. I had only managed to bring so many things over with me in my one case and, as I'd never really gone to parties before and had never been interested in fashion, I was a bit worried.

I found a pair of jeans and a t-shirt that I'd brought with me and decided to wear them. I was wracked with nerves. I had never had so many people want to be friends with me before. How should I act with them? What should I do in conversations? I ended up having to go out for a walk. There was no privacy in the apartment.

I walked all the way down to Central to meet up with Matt trying to calm myself down.

We met at the usual meet place; the ledge next to the ATMs on Pedder Street. He led me down to the junction of Pedder Street and Des Voeux Road where we jumped on a tram to Causeway Bay. We sat up on the top floor where Matt told me loads of stories, most of them very funny.

He said that just a couple of weeks previously, he had been on a tram with his mate Mark when someone had been run over by a tram going in the opposite direction and was dragged along the road.

Okay, so not all his stories were funny.

We got off at a huge department store called Sogo and we quickly found a shirt and a pair of trousers. I still had money coming in from the Navy which I was transferring into my HSBC account. The store was cheap so I could buy what I wanted.

Back on the tram again and heading back towards the central district, we passed through Wan Chai. Matt had warned me about this place. Full of strip clubs, gangsters and drug users, he said. He said people got mugged and killed there all the time. Once he said he was there when the American Navy was in town and he and his mate got beaten up by five of them. He told me that I should never go there as it was too dangerous. There were drug dealers on every corner, he said.

He then told me how there was generally a drugs bust every year or so at school, usually because someone had overdosed or died. He said a girl had died last year at the back of the Inn Place. I didn't know whether to believe him or not as he was full of lots of stories, but I said that I would bear it in mind.

By the time we had finished chatting, we were back in Central. Getting off the tram, he took me into a huge office building called the Worldwide Trade Centre. The first few floors were full of small shops and he took me to a heavy metal rock shop that sold leather clothes, earrings, studs, posters. You name it, this tiny little shop had it. Looking through the jewellery Matt turned to me.

'Do you want to get our ears pierced'?

I'd never thought about it before but said yes.

'Come on', he said, as led me along the corridors of shops.

'My sister got her ears pierced here last week.'

We found the shop he was looking for and bought a set of gold ear studs. One for each of us.

We went outside and sat at the side of the ATMs where we had met earlier. I didn't really know what to do. Matt told me to just push the sharp bit through my ear and said it was easy. So, I did it. There was a little bit of resistance, but I managed to push it straight through with little effort. Sticking the clasp onto the back of the stud, I could feel my ear tingle a bit but when I put my fingers to it there was no blood and I felt a wee wave of strange contentment and accomplishment wash over me.

Matt wasn't as relaxed about it as I was. He seemed to be taking an age saying he wanted to get it in the correct position. His hands were shaking when he finally pressed the stud against his left ear. In the late 80s, a stud in the right ear meant that you were gay.

What followed was an hour of screams and bleeding because on his first attempt, he only managed to push the stud through slightly before he stopped pushing and pulled it out instead. This caused the bleeding to start and by the time he had fought through the pain and his quickly swelling lobe, blood was everywhere and hiding the gold stud he had so wanted to have.

We parted ways, me feeling ultra cool with my new jewellery, he felt a little bit throbby. We would meet again for the party after we had both been home to change.

As soon as I got home my mum saw the stud and told me to take it out immediately because my dad would go mad. I was 16 so I just ignored her. I went for a shower in the horrid little bathroom, shaved, squeezed any annoying spots, smothered myself in deodorant and aftershave put my new clothes on and was out the door before my mum could say another word to me.

I went up and waited on Conduit Road for the small white and green minibus that would take me all the way down to the final stop outside HMS Tamar. It was an irregular service; not one with a timetable. The bus would wait until it had enough people on board and then set off. The roads down the hill were steep, and it sounded like the gearbox would explode at any moment, sending shards of fragmented gears flying. Even with gears and brakes screaming, we made it down the hill successfully.

I was glad I was getting off at the last stop as I hadn't yet mastered what you needed to shout out whenever you wanted to get off the bus.

'Ni do, m'goy' [here please], as I later learnt to shout.

Queen's Pier, where the boat would be leaving for the party, was a two-minute walk from the bus stop, opposite the Hong Kong City Hall.

As I turned the corner onto the paved area that ran along next to the harbour wall, I saw a large group of teenagers, but my eyes were immediately drawn to the boat. Wow, it was a proper Chinese junk with massive brown sails. It looked incredible! I couldn't believe that after just one week at the school, I was going to a party on such a thing. I joined the group. Matt didn't show up, I found out later that his ear wouldn't allow him!

At the command of the birthday girl's dad, we all climbed aboard.

There were buckets of beer everywhere. There must also have been food, but I didn't notice it. The junk manoeuvred itself away from the pier and into the mass of other boats, large and small, that swarmed around this part of the harbour. We headed west. Everyone was chatting, laughing and downing beers.

I was leaning on the rail staring out at one of the most stunning views on the planet. It was a mixture of organic and non-organic. The huge skyscrapers lit up with the mountains just a faint but always present hugeness behind.

Small, wooden boats had whole families living on them. Dad at the bow with a long bamboo pole with a net picking up anything recyclable, beer cans thrown by some of my shipmates and plastic bottles. Halfway down the tiny craft, mum was hanging the washing and, under a canopy at the stern, a couple of children doing their homework, oblivious to the rich kids sailing past throwing their empty cans to their father for sport.

As we left the main part of the harbour, the view opened out so that you could see many different islands dotted around. Some had lights so I knew they were inhabited; some did not. One of these was a prison, I was told. How terrifying that must be, I thought, as all the islands looked foreboding, covered in thick jungle and jagged rock faces.

We passed some huge container ships, anchored and waiting their turn to enter the harbour and pick up containers full of Christmas gifts that would sit under millions of Western Christmas trees. Those kids would probably only be excited with their new toys for a day or two. I wondered what the kids living on the wee wooden boat would get.

The night turned into a drunken mess. Kids got thrown off the junk from time to time. I got so pissed, I ended the trip throwing up in the toilet. There was a mess everywhere. It was a junk party, after all.

第十一章

The days blurred into one and then another until the day of my trial arrived. The police had been into see me a few times asking questions. Who did I get the heroin from? Where was I going with it? Who did I do the robberies with? Who were my accomplices? If I gave them names, they would see if I could get a lighter sentence. A lighter sentence … what was that, a death sentence? The prison was full of triads; you wouldn't last long if you were a grass in here.

So, the trial came and I pleaded not guilty. The court looked at the evidence and found me guilty.

DC 21612

My new number was a transitional number. The DC stood for 'detention centre'. You could be sentenced to DC; it was everyone's dream unless, of course, they were found not guilty. Being sentenced to the detention centre meant just a 1-year sentence. It was a tough sentence as they made you work hard, a bit like hard labour.

The DCs who had been there for a while all looked healthy and fit. If they followed the rules, they could be out after just 6 months. All of us waiting to be sentenced dreamed of a DC sentence. I was realistic. I had overheard some conversations with my limited Cantonese that for my crimes I would be looking at ten years.

After the verdict, before I was sentenced, I was given a grey uniform and placed in limbo in a small and cramped room in the detention centre part of the prison. I spent the entire day there. Knees and shoulders touching the guys to the left and right of you. Knees bent up touching someone's arse in front and someone's feet touching your arse behind.

Rows and rows of prisoners all with their thoughts in the darkest of places, wondering what would be happening to them. No exercise, no reading, no TV, no this, no that. No idea of how long the wait would be.

Some had been there for months with no end in sight. It depended on the complexity of the case. There was the occasional meeting that we attended so that pre-sentence reports could be prepared. This at least broke the monotony. These reports looked at factors such as the impact on society that you had made, whether there were any mitigating factors and if you had shown any remorse.

We ate all our meals in that room as well. That was enough to turn the strongest stomach. The only relief was when we were finally deposited back into our cells. We were always the first to go back. I have no idea what time it was but it was two hours before the remands and the prisoners.

Short-term cells are always the worst. The shorter the period you expected to spend there, the less care you took of your living space. Added to that, we were never given anything to clean them. The one I was in was filthy. Without even the smallest of rags, there was nothing I could do about it.

I tried not to look too closely or to think about it but there were all kinds of bodily fluids covering the walls. Someone had used their shit to draw around the toilet. The sink had dirt on it so thick that the water had carved a channel through it.

All we could do for those hours before lights out was sit there thinking to ourselves. I was the only one in a single cell. At least all the other guys were in pairs. That would have helped to pass the time if your cellmate wasn't completely mental, which many of them were.

One evening whilst I was sitting on my bed leaning against the cold concrete wall, an officer came to my cell. Without saying anything, he placed some papers between the bars of the front of my cell and walked away.

It had only been four months, but I was already quite institutionalised. So, I just sat there looking at what he had left not really knowing what to do. It took a while to finally have the courage to reach over and take the papers. I leant back, staring at what I had in my hands. It was a letter, the first letter I had received. It was from Asanki.

When I went back to court for sentencing, I was very surprised, shocked and embarrassed to see one of my former teachers, Mr Forse, in the court. I didn't get a chance to speak to him but the feelings I experienced seeing him there will never leave me. It made me realise that I was good enough for someone to care about me. It gave me hope which stayed with me throughout my sentence.

I heard the judge sentence me to a total of six years. I can't remember hearing anything else. It was only when I was returned to the prison that I discovered that there were separate sentences for each charge and the judge had made them concurrent, so the total sentence was actually three years.

I also found out that I would be released after two-thirds of my sentence. I worked out that my release date would be two days before my twentieth birthday because 1992 was a leap year. I had already spent sixty-four days in prison, so I had 666 days to go. That was as long as I didn't have any time added on for bad behaviour.

Young Prisoner 90760

When I was returned to the prison after my sentencing, I was given the much-coveted brown uniform and led up to the cell block which held convicted prisoners. It was much cleaner than what I had previously experienced: the hallways, the bars on the windows and the cells. The cell I was shown into was slightly dusty but everything worked: water in the tap, a flushing toilet and a sturdy bed. The mattress was the worst part, it stank. I realised that this was where I was going to spend the next two years of my life.

Something changed in me that night. Something that wasn't good. I had crazy dreams that I was going to take over the prison, that I would take control of everyone. They wouldn't be difficult to control. They were all morons. They were all petty criminals that didn't have any smarts amongst them. I would start tomorrow as soon as I got out of my cell. I would have the attitude that I was the boss rather than them.

I had flipped. My brain had gone into meltdown.

Chapter Eleven

Each day, after school, I would rarely go home straight away and would instead head down the hill to McDonald's. There were a group of us that followed the same routine: McDonald's; a walk around central and then up to Thingummy's.

By the time we got to Thingummy's, there were just a handful of us left, sometimes it was just me. But whenever I got down the stairs, there were always a bunch of friendly faces to greet me.

Peter, the manager, would immediately pour me a pint when he saw me and speak to me in Cantonese. I would smile and nod and go and sit with my friends. There, I would stay most of the night with maybe an outing or two to the nearest 7-Eleven to get something to eat, generally noodles or a tuna sandwich.

If it was a friend's birthday, we would head up to one of the pubs or clubs in Lan Kwai Fong and spend the night there. These were just the weekdays. At the weekends we would usually head to one of the beaches where we would take our own beer and dance on the beach until we either got the last bus home or we all shared a taxi.

One night in Thingummy's, I was sitting in my usual spot getting drunk with a new guy I'd met recently, also called Stuart. With a black leather jacket with 'The Dead Kennedys' across the back, I liked him instantly. He told me about various situations that he'd found himself in and that he sometimes didn't know how he had got out of. I was starting to learn more and more about the dark side of Hong Kong.

'They call me Seh Gi, snake boy', he said.

'Who calls you that?'

'The triad mate, the triad. Stay away from them, they're really bad news.'

Stuart went up to the bar, got the jukebox key from Peter and threw it to me so that I could unlock the jukebox and with a flick of a switch, add loads of free credits.

A special treat for his best customers, I was becoming one of them. I threw the key back to Stuart and was waiting for two pints of San Miguel to be poured for us when a young Chinese guy came and sat next to me. He was older than us, didn't say anything but laughed when others laughed and acted like he was part of the Thingummy's group. He was a big lad and looked like he worked out, but a nice guy. After a while and a few more beers, he nudged me.

'I'm Lennon'.

'Hi'.

'I want to learn English; you help me?'

Well, me being me I said, 'Why not'.

And that was that. For the rest of the night, we chatted, and I shared some phrases in English with him. He picked it all up very quickly, his English wasn't that bad.

When he got up at one point to go to the toilet Stuart sat closer to me.

'Stay away from the Chinese guys mate, I'm serious, they're big trouble, stay safe', he said.

When Lennon came back Stuart moved a bit further away again and sat there quietly.

The next night I was in again and there was Lennon. He bought me drinks all night and our friendship continued. I didn't think Stuart could have been talking about this guy. Lennon seemed all right; he didn't look like someone who was a part of the Chinese mafia.

If he was, why would he be hanging out here with all these foreigners?

第12章

When I woke up, it was still dark. I lay on my bed trying to think, trying to remember all the crazy dreams I'd had during the night. There were brief flickers of dreams. One I could remember was of me just giving in to everything and killing someone, anyone who annoyed me.

To become an animal in prison. To give up all the societal norms that I had learnt over the years. I thought of my friends, my life outside, where I had gone so wrong. That thought was the one that would stay with me and be a constant companion over the next twelve months of the hell that was about to follow.

I had thought that I would be joining the population that day, but I was in for yet another surprise because all newly sentenced prisoners had to go through a week of induction. Basically, we were made to clean the prison. From sun-up to sundown, we were scrubbing and sweeping.

Everywhere we went, I was getting stared at. Prisoners getting moved from one place to the next would all be staring at me. We were made to eat our food separately from the rest and I was made to sit separately even from my induction group. Each morning, we were marched silently into the dining hall. I was always made to be last. When I got to the first shutter, the same routine as before I was sentenced.

'On Chaan'.

I never was able to drink the tea. I tried a few times when thirst overtook my senses. Always cold and disgusting, with the floaty bit. The same old bread and the dry slice of cheese. I managed to force it down. I lost a lot of weight in those early weeks.

For lunch, the local guys would get either sweet green congee or rice soup. The green congee always smelled amazing and I longed for it. I got the same as breakfast. At dinner time the others got another plate full of rice with vegetables, and occasionally some bits of chicken wing or other indescribable meat. They would also get an orange. An orange! Despite my previous hatred of them, my mouth now watered when I saw them. When they all started peeling them after finishing their rice, the smell filled the whole dining hall. It was intoxicating.

My dinner was the same old thing, tea and a plate of what you would normally throw away when making dinner: potatoes that had more black parts than white, the offcuts of vegetables: the root of a cabbage; the ends of carrots; and a piece of meat that was tougher than any leather shoes I had ever owned.

We were worked very hard during the day so I would have eaten the plate if I had been able to. I was never a big vegetable fan outside but I managed to force everything down. The other prisoners continued to stare at me all the way through meals as well.

I felt a deep foreboding. The only reason why nothing happened was because the guards ran the place so tightly and anyone who caused the slightest bit of noise would be dragged from their chair and battered by a group of them.

No talking, stay in line, do exactly as you are told or suffer the consequences. There were some mentally challenged prisoners amongst us and the guards used them for their own amusement. Sometimes they would call one of them over and then give them a beating because they had got up out of their seat.

There were often fights, sometimes over the slightest things. The fights didn't last long because of the pleasure the guards got in wading in and swinging their batons around.

It had been a very long time since I had spoken to anyone. No one spoke to me in English, even though most of the guards wore the red flash under their number to say that they could. I bumped into another prisoner once and without the aid of language we got into a fight when a simple argument could have solved everything. That time we weren't seen by the guards so we got away with it but that was the last time I did.

The week of the induction came to an end and I was finally allowed to eat with everyone else. The prisoners were split into two groups, A and B. The two foreigners that I had seen before were in group A and I was put into group B. This meant that I was never able to be with them.

Chapter Twelve

Acting as the gentleman, I bought Rosie a corsage and got a taxi to her house to pick her up. She was in my law class and I had asked her to the prom. She was very pretty with curly brown hair and smart. She wasn't part of the party crowd either, which was just perfect.

This should have been a big deal; I would be meeting her family and would have to be very polite. However, this was not a big deal for me because, deep down, that was who I really was.

She looked beautiful in a dark blue dress with puffy sleeves and a tight waist with the hem filling out down to her knees. Beautiful indeed. I was feeling very dapper in the tuxedo Blakey had helped me pick out to hire.

We got into a taxi and went straight to the Hilton Hotel where the dance was taking place. What a sight it was. All the guys were in tuxedos and all the girls were in amazing dresses. Loads of dancing, twirling and jigging.

A dancing competition was held later in the evening so Rosie and I jumped onto the dance floor. I wasn't really paying much attention to anyone else; I was simply enchanted by how gorgeous Rosie looked.

At one point I looked around and there were only a few couples left on the dance floor. Others had been asked to leave the floor and those of us who remained danced it out to see who would be crowned king and queen of the prom.

Up until that moment, I had been completely relaxed but now, with the light on us, I began to freeze with nervousness. Rosie expertly calmed me down and we started dancing together again as if we had been born dancers. To my absolute astonishment, we were suddenly the only couple left on the dance floor with huge cheers going up all around us. Rosie and I were king and queen of the prom. I couldn't take it in. From being one of the most despised people in my last school to being the king of the prom within the same year. We had to go up to the DJ and accept our prize which was a lunch for four at the Hilton on a Sunday.

What a buzz. When the dance finished, Rosie had to go home but I decided to stay on with my pals and ended up going to Lan Kwai Fong where we all danced away looking amazing in our prom outfits. It was a great night. One I won't forget. The night when I was made a king.

第十三章

I was allocated to the television repair workshop. It was a long narrow room with workbenches along each side and one long one in the middle. I walked in and fifty pairs of eyes turned on me, with not one smile amongst them. They just sat there and stared as if sizing up their prey.

I felt vulnerable; we were locked in the room with just one guard who was called 'Sifu' [teacher]. He was a strange little fellow, with bulging eyes and a humped back. But he was the only person to smile at me for months and welcomed me. He seemed happy to see me. It almost caused me to well up. Almost, but not quite.

Showing weakness here, I reckoned, was the same as showing fear to a dog, I would be bitten. He showed me around the workshop and where I was to sit. So, I sat.

There was no talking out loud, but whispers back and forth between the other prisoners, all the while never taking their eyes off me. I watched Sifu fixing a TV with another prisoner who seemed oblivious to my presence.

We sat there all morning, me watching Sifu, them watching me. Then it was lunch and we were marched to the dining hall where I collected my tea, cheese and bread and sat down. Five hundred pairs of eyes watching me eat my lunch.

I noticed that lunch today was white congee and hardly any of them took any. For them to not eat it, it must have been bad. Then I noticed that they weren't just staring at me, but they were staring at my food as well. What was unsatisfying for me was something they hadn't had in a long time, and they wanted it.

At the end of lunch, those who had had the congee walked past me to return their cups. They walked as close to me as possible. There was some muttering under breaths as they passed. I couldn't make most of it out but there were some words I did understand.

'Diu lay Gwai Gi' [fuck you, foreign devil] was unmistakable.

In the afternoon, I was taken to the classrooms. As this was a young offender's unit, prisoners had to go to class once a day. Each class held about fifteen prisoners and one teacher/guard. As I walked down the corridor, the small, barred opening to the classrooms was full of staring faces.

I was taken to the last classroom. This classroom, I soon found out, was for the second-highest security prisoners. The serious bad asses. I was put into it because I was deemed to be a high risk. Although my charges and convicted offences were only category B, I was seen as a category A prisoner due to the prison's risk assessment.

We were all kept away from the extremely serious crazies, the ones who would bite your face off if they got a chance.

In fact, it was a lucky break for me to be put in with this lot. They were the very long-term prisoners; the shortest sentence was about 15 years, so they had been in for a while and were a lot more subdued than the short-term guys.

I sat down next to one guy. He was about the same age as me but there was an air of depression surrounding him. He hardly ever looked up from his desk. We all sat at desks but only a few were doing any work; the others were just sitting talking. This was the only place in the whole prison where you could sit down and have a conversation with the other prisoners as it was a classroom and talking was permitted.

A skinny little Chinese guy walked over to my table:

'I speak English. I double murderer, I double murderer'.

He seemed pleased with himself. His English was poor but with my crap Chinese, I was able to work out that he had robbed a travel agency and stuck a screwdriver through the throats of both the members of staff. Seemed that there was no need to do it, but he found himself doing it anyway. He even did it after he had got the money. He had been sentenced to a full life sentence but was waiting for his appeal.

Others were in for acid attacks where they had thrown acid onto their ex-girlfriends or even just girls that had refused their advances. There were a lot of murderers. My new desk mate, whose English name was Stephen, was doing a full life term for murder. It was then that I discovered murderers are the least cause for concern in a prison as their acts occurred mostly out of the blue or under the influence of alcohol or drugs which aren't available in the prison.

His story was sad and you could see it reflected in his whole personality. Two schools met up to have a fight, as many do around the world. He couldn't even remember the argument that had brought them together. Then the fight happened, a few kids got hurt but everyone went home. Unfortunately, one went home with a head injury and died three days later.

Stephen had hit him over the head with a stick causing a blood clot in the brain. Because Stephen had taken the stick with him to where the fight was going to take place, he was charged with premeditated murder. Although he had been given a full life term, he was hoping to be freed after 18 years as he was 15 years old at the time of the offence.

Fuck. On one hand, you have a twisted fuck like Mr Double Murderer and then you have Stephen. The whole room was full of these kinds of stories. But most importantly for me, the classroom was the only place where I felt relatively safe.

I started to think about trying to do a course or something. I was going to be there for at least two years so it would be useful to get myself qualified for something when I was finally released.

At the end of the day, we marched again to the dining hall for dinner.

Chapter Thirteen

The partying got harder and harder the closer to Christmas we got. I had met many people now who had their own flats so had been spending a lot of time staying with friends. There was little point going home. No bed to sleep in made friends' places somewhat of a better proposition.

Particularly when my dad was home, it was just horrendous. I thought that his promotion may have made life a bit better. But now that he was home most of the time instead of working away, his drinking was a constant as well as my mum's.

The times I tried to stay at home in the evening, sitting there watching TV with them drinking their Whisky and Bacardi, was just not fun. Even if I was tired, I couldn't go to bed because my bed was the couch where they sat for at least 6 hours every night drinking.

Then, because he was hungover in the morning, he would come into the living room and start shouting at me, calling me a lazy bastard and to get out of bed and get to school, whilst my mum, bleary-eyed, would stagger into the kitchen to try and make breakfast. She would be so all over the place, and the kitchen so small that I couldn't get in there to make myself anything. So, I usually left the house without having anything to eat at all.

Sometimes I had to take money out of her purse so that I could buy some food at school and pay for my McDonalds and for drinks in Thingummy's later. Since I was such a regular customer, I had a tab. I paid it once a week with what was left of my money from the Navy and whenever my mum gave me some money. I think she gave me money mostly so that I could stay out of the house, she always said.

'Anything for an easy life'.

There was no life at home anymore and I just didn't want to be there. My brother had his own room, so he could hide in there but I know it was affecting him too.

On Christmas Eve that year, I just didn't go home. I didn't go home until 5.00 am on 5 January.

But before that, it was New Year. I had been staying at different friends' houses. So many of my friends had families with a lot of money. They didn't just have a bedroom, most of them had a separate part of the house with a lounge and everything, so it was easy to crash at theirs. Also, a lot of their parents worked away. Empty houses party time!

Some of their families had even left them in Hong Kong whilst they went home to their own countries for the holidays, leaving my friends in the capable hands of the 'amahs' [housemaids] and drivers.

Sometimes, someone's driver would come and pick us up in the family's limo and drive us about: McDonald's; 7/11; Lan Kwai Fong; wherever we needed to go. These friends had money, not just money, but a lot of money. Most parents chose to deal with their guilt of not seeing their kids by giving them tons of money.

On Christmas Day itself, Rosie and I went with our friend onto his dad's company's yacht. His dad was the chairman of HSBC so the yacht was amazing as you can imagine.

I can't remember all the parties that I went to. I didn't see Rosie at all after Christmas Day and, to be honest, we had pretty much split up by then. So, on New Year's Eve, I met up with friends at Thingummy's to start the night's celebrations. It was incredible. That was the night that I became a man, I think.

Within the first hour, I was screwing this redhead from a different school in the rat-infested alley next to Thingummy's. Incredible, as I have said. Just casual sex, no condoms were discussed.

And she wasn't the only one. By the end of the night, I had had sex with three different girls and snogged six at least. I wasn't the only one to be doing this. It was mental. I remember at one point walking up to 7-Eleven to get more cigarettes and practically having to step over two teenagers who were on top of each other in the middle of the street. It was mental. We left Thingummy's and staggered up to Lan Kwai Fong. Then someone shouted:

'You want to Tria Fuck?'

'What?' I said, rubbing my ears.

'Tria Fuck, you want to go Tria Fuck?'

Still looking confused, one of my mates said, 'Friar Tucks'.

It was a pub around the corner on Icehouse Street. Laughing, we headed towards this new pub with the hilarious name.

As soon as I stepped inside, I saw her. She was sensational.

I don't know what it was about her, but she shocked me sober.

She took my breath away; I just stood and stared at her. She was the most beautiful person I had ever seen in my life.

She turned and saw me. She locked her eyes on me and, what was this, she came towards me, smiling? She took my hand, led me over to a table and kissed me. What the hell, what was going on? This couldn't be possible.

'You don't know me, do you?'

She asked between breaths and kissing.

'I know you; I was there at the prom trying to get your attention, and you don't remember seeing me do you'.

'No, I don't sorry?'

She kissed me again.

'You want to know my name?'

'It's Allison'.

And she started kissing me again, she wouldn't stop. I don't know if I got a drink in the pub but soon my friends were telling me we had to go. I was being wrestled out of the door with Allison still stuck to my face.

We were on the street before she let go.

I just looked at her, in total shock as my friends dragged me away. What was I doing? I was heading away from heaven. At 16 years old, I was overcome. Overcome with her energy, her amazing energy. And then I was around the corner, and she was gone.

Eventually, I had to go home. At 5 am on 5 January, I collapsed on the couch only to be woken by my dad two hours later.

'Shit, here we go', I thought.

Thinking that I was going to get a complete battering from him. I suppose it would show he cared, so that would be positive. But no, I was wrong.

'You have to get up at 7 am because you're playing cricket'.

I'd completely forgotten that my Australian mate nicknamed Didge [short for didgeridoo] who was captain of the school's cricket B team had asked me to play in the school cricket competition today.

So, I jumped up and grabbed the things I needed, stuffed them into a bag and headed for the school where I was getting picked up.

I was in an absolute state having been constantly drinking since 24 December. That had been the most I had drunk and for the longest time, it's amazing what the human body can withstand.

I don't remember much of the day, only the last game when I was so wiped out that I couldn't bowl straight to save my life and gave away fifteen runs!

We had made it to the final and were playing the South Island School basketball team, but we lost, mostly due to my bowling. Melanie and a couple of other friends had shown up for the final game and so as soon as the last run was scored and the last ball had been bowled, I quickly got changed and left, not even bothering to wait for the award ceremony. I so desperately now needed a drink and to be back in my safe place, Thingummy's.

That's where we started but we quickly headed to the In Place where the barmaid Eddy gave me a special birthday gift on the fire escape stairs. It was such a lovely treat that I headed back to her place afterwards and spent the night with her again.

So that was my 17th birthday: cricketing, drinking, clubbing, sexing with a barmaid, how can birthdays get any better than this?

第十四章

The first wage I got was HK$2 [16p] which enabled me to buy a packet of biscuits. It was the first treat I had had in months. It was a small packet of six round biscuits with a cream filling. They were called Sisisik.

To hold that prize in my hand was amazing. I sat in my cell that night and handled the packet for about an hour deciding whether to desecrate it by opening it. I just couldn't wait any longer. I was imagining the taste, the feeling of the biscuits and the cream in my mouth. I tried to smell them through the packet and dreamt that I could.

I opened the packet a tiny bit at first and immediately brought it up to my nose. The smell filled and emptied my stomach in a moment, I'm sure jets of saliva shot out my mouth and perhaps I even became slightly aroused. I opened the packet more, slowly making sure that the ends that had been heated together were peeled apart so gently as not to rip. To rip this packet would be abusive, abusive to the upcoming joy. If the packet had ripped, the whole experience would have been damaged, as if I had disrespected the moment, the encounter with the sweetness.

Once the packet's ends had been perfectly separated, I sat back on my bed and had to make a tough decision. Should I bite through all three layers at once? I would feel the top biscuit breaking against my top teeth, the lower biscuit crunching against my lower teeth and eventually I would feel the cream through the debris of the broken biscuit. Or, should I pull the two top layers apart and take the cream first by licking it gently? I had to make the decision before I could take this fondant-filled orgasm out of its erotically decadent packaging. I sat back again; I just couldn't decide.

These were the first biscuits that I'd had in six months and I would not be getting any more for at least another month. These ponderings were painful. It was also constantly on my mind that my life could be ended at any moment: the sharpened point of a chopstick could be rammed into my cranial areas; a sharpened piece of a toothbrush with, perhaps, a razor blade melted into it might be dragged purposefully across my neck, opening my throat and gullet wide enough to deposit one of the Sisisik biscuits. That was it; if they were going to kill me then I should just go for it. And so, with the passion of a wild animal which has scented the opposite sex and is greedy for lust-filled rutting, I did.

I grabbed the first piece of joy and shoved it into my mouth. I crunched it as if I was a grazing animal and it was my grass. Every crunch threw shivers of orgasmic passion through my body. My mouth filled with saliva. It was a multiple orgasm, waves and waves of pleasure coursing through the facial area. Nerve endings danced with joy.

I fell back on my bed, spent. The biscuit had been expertly crunched for the longest any biscuit had been before and or would be in the future. Every piece of it was admired, loved and thanked for the joy it brought me that night in my dark, damp hell hole.

Not only was I thankful for the biscuit; I was thankful to myself. For putting so much effort into the act of mastication, so much thought. I would never do so again. That would be the peak of my mastication efforts, the finest thing that I would ever put in my mouth. For it wasn't just a biscuit; it was what it stood for.

It stood for hope. It stood for effort, earnings and energy spent. It stood for survival and saying 'fuck you' to all who had tried to kill me or make me kill myself or anyone else, for that matter. I had taken back control. I could decide whether to crunch or pull apart and I decided that I would no longer pull things apart; I would tackle them head-on. I would stick a whole biscuit in my mouth as a sign of defiance.

This went through my head like a steam train. I was having a sugar rush that was giving me delusions of grandeur that would not last. The light went from my cell again and I remembered where I was but I also realised that I had five more biscuits left!

Chapter Fourteen

On the first day back at school, the front hall was filled with students. I can't remember why but there were names on boards in the hallway, it could have been for exams or something. But the whole school seemed to be filling the space. People were greeting each other after the holidays and all the excited voices made it noisy. It was difficult to make yourself heard.

I was looking around for my friends when something magical happened. As I turned to my right, it was as, if on command, all the students in front of me started to part. First, the ones right next to me then the next ones and the next, like some kind of strange human domino effect. I stood there staring at what was happening. Then it was as if a bright light shone from nowhere and there she was standing right in front of me.

It was as if I was seeing an angel. My whole being turned to jelly; it felt overwhelming. She was standing there smiling at me and I started to smile back. We moved together as if on a moving walkway, hers towards me and mine towards her. And then we were together. No words would come to me; I stood there in amazement and awe at this incredibly beautiful girl standing in front of me giving off all the energy that I was feeling. She was as I was. We were the same. I couldn't speak, she couldn't speak. It was her; it was Allison.

Then one of her friends, Beverly, whispered in my ear.
'Ask her for her number'.
'Can I have your number?'
I barely got the words out.
'Yes, it's 5226160'.

Then the crowd started to close in on us again, the school bell went and she disappeared.

In hindsight, I should have given her Thingummy's number [5241075], as this year I'd be making it my home.

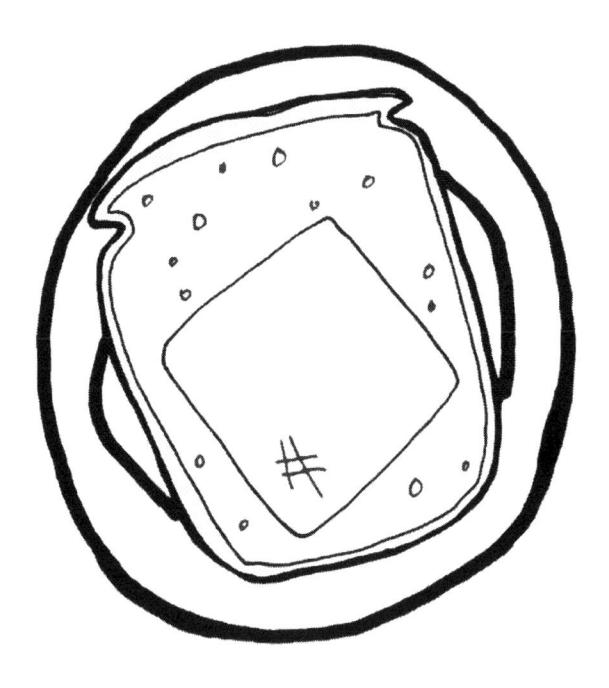

第十五章

A few days turned into a few weeks. Nothing really changed. Then one day, I was sitting in the dining hall having just got my dinner when a guy ran over and stole my plate. I was in a state of stunned shock. Firstly, how did he get away with it? Secondly, if I did something in retaliation, what would be the result?

I just sat there, dumbfounded. Then, when back in my cell, I tried to work out what to do. The guy who had taken my plate was a guy who was always hanging around with the top guy in the prison. He was called the big brother and the other guy, the little brother. These terms were triad related. The guy who took my plate must have known that the guards wouldn't have done anything as he was the little brother. I imagine that everything had been planned for days.

The next morning at breakfast, the same thing happened again. He sneaked up behind my seat and stole my bread and cheese. I was already starving from not having had anything to eat the night before. This time I couldn't hold my rage back, I leapt to my feet but before I could reach him, the guards jumped me and held me down for my first official beating. I was dragged to the floor, and they laid into me with their batons. I was then dragged to the governor's office where I was told that I wasn't allowed to get out of my seat. I considered telling him what happened, but I knew that was grassing and my life would not be worth living. So, I said nothing, took the telling off and went to my workshop.

At lunchtime, I could just tell that something was coming. Standing in the queue waiting to get served, a guy deliberately knocked me. I turned around and squared up to him. He screamed something in my face and pushed me. I had nothing to say and pushed him back, harder. But before anything else could happen, a guard appeared between us.

He pushed us apart, sent me to the back of the queue, and let us continue to get our lunch things. But this was it; I had a feeling that something was coming. They were starting to size me up. I looked over to the table where the big brother was sitting and stared at him. He was staring back with the little brother talking excitedly in his ear.

The big brother nodded and the little brother got up and walked towards my table. I looked around and saw that none of the guards were looking but every prisoner was. As he neared my table, I readied myself for an attack. It didn't come but as he passed me, he whispered in English 'We going to kill you'.

I believed him.

Chapter Fifteen

The first couple of weeks of the year at school were filled with mock exams, the ones you take before the real ones in the summer. As my dad was at home and he and my mum had taken up their drinking places on my bed, I spent nearly every night either at Thingummy's or at a friend's house. So, it's fair to say that absolutely no studying had been done for any of my exams.

Surprisingly, I got 80 per cent in my business exam, 77 per cent in maths but 22 per cent in law. I think it was because it was more commercial law that we were doing. I would have preferred criminal law, I thought to myself whilst sitting in Thingummy's counting the zeros that some clever artist had graffitied onto the wall trying to represent the number of brain cells that had been lost in this fine establishment.

Weekends were spent mostly hanging out with my new sidekick Melanie. As we were both new, we found ourselves exploring the place more and more together. We spent time at the Peak Café enjoying a coffee whilst looking out over the view. We'd chat mostly about who we were or were not seeing or fancying. She had started seeing Andy, the guy whose dad worked at the bank. He had just passed his driving test but she had dumped him.

Other days after school it was either straight to McDonald's or to the video game arcade where I sat and played Tetris for hours and hours whilst others fought long battles against each other on the street fighter machine. One lad would sit on the stool, take his shoe off one foot and challenge to beat anyone with his toes. And he did beat them.

I didn't eat at home anymore; I was slowly going through the local convenience store's selection of snacks that could be eaten straight from the fridge or those that you could heat up in the microwaves provided or with the boiling water for the noodle cups. Sometimes I'd eat out at one of the amazing street cafés that you could find down the alleyways of Central. Food was cheap, fresh and delicious. I certainly wasn't malnourished. I probably had a healthier diet than I did at home, apart from the huge amount of beer I now drank. I did occasionally drink a spirit or five but I was predominantly on the beer.

Although I didn't see it with my own eyes, I did hear that there were a lot of other things going on as well but I just wasn't interested. I had never seen drugs before. Of course, I knew what they were, especially hashish, but I had no interest in any of them.

Sitting in Thingummy's, I'd notice the same people disappearing every so often outside for a joint or whatever. There was a small park half way between the bar and the 7-Eleven store. When we walked past, you would catch a glimpse of some people in the darkness doing their drugs. We never went in, it looked far too dodgy.

Some of my fellow drinkers must have been around 14; they started young. The number of unconscious kids that would be found outside the bar every weekend and even sometimes during the week was disturbing. Some would be taken home by friends while others were taken to the hospital.

You would also hear of some being arrested for being too drunk or for not having their Hong Kong Identity Cards with them which was a legal requirement.

Our parents and the schools must have known about this. I am sure that the schools 100 per cent knew that their underage students were out drinking and partying all the time, simply because some of the teachers were doing it as well.

One night the school sent a minibus full of teachers to Kowloon where they parked near the In Place. Each time a student came outside they grabbed them, took them to the minibus and made them sit inside while they called their parents. The fire escape was busier than the dance floor that night!

第十六章

'He kill two of your friends.'

One day sitting in the classroom on the first floor, the Category As walked past our door as usual. The acid boy leaned next to me and whispered, 'He kill two of your friends.'

'What?'

'He kill two of your friends.'

'What do you mean?' I said,

'That guy who walks past kill two foreign school kids with his friend, a long time back.'

It suddenly clicked in my brain. Could he be serious? It made sense though. I was in a maximum-security prison and the Cat As are the worst of the worst. What he was saying was that one of the guys who walked past our classroom twice a day was responsible for the brutal rape and murder of two kids who went to my school a few years previously.

My thoughts instantly went to retaliation. It was the most powerful feeling I'd had in months, finally drowning out the fear of attack, the intense depression of loneliness and the lack of any sort of control I had in my life.

My mind went straight to how I could get him. It was nearly impossible. We were always locked up when they were outside to be kept safe from the sadistic killers that were housed in a block -- the prison within the prison. Twice a day they would walk past and the next time I would get acid boy to point out exactly who it was.

I waited, staring at the door for the rest of the day. My focus was on seeing which one it was. My mind planning how I would avenge in some way the terrible event that he and his other animal friends had perpetrated. I didn't even know the kids that he'd killed but that didn't matter. They went to my school; my friends had known them. The events would never be forgotten at school.

I knew the time was coming when they would be taken out of their segregated classroom and back to their high-security safety. I got the acid boy to sit next to me and to point him out to me, my prey.

When I could hear the footsteps as they approached, my skin started to crawl, thinking that I was going to come face-to-face with one of the monsters. As they went past, acid boy pointed.

'Him'.

He looked into our classroom, our eyes locked and my intense hatred flew across the room in my gaze. He saw it. He knew.

From that day onward, his face was burned into my conscious memory. I would see him at least twice a day, sometimes more. He always looked at me glaring at him. I could feel - sense his discomfort. He knew that I knew. He understood that my only goal in life now was to get the chance to attack him, to harm him.

I had no concerns about what would happen to me, what the guards would do to me and what sanctions I would get. I would happily spend the rest of my sentence in solitary confinement just to get one chance to get my hands on him. I would hurt him as badly as I could.

I would have just seconds to attack. I couldn't risk a weapon. I didn't want to get caught with one and to never get the chance to attack him. The chance I would get would come out of the blue. I would be unprepared for it as it would have to happen by accident, a hundred different circumstances all coming together at one moment when I, a Cat B prisoner would mistakenly be in the same area as the Cat A prisoners. So, I waited. I glared every day, every week and every month. I would be ready for the chance when it came.

When the chance did arrive, I wasn't in the classroom. The police had visited me again to ask me more questions. A waste of time. I think they just wanted me to take the rap for other crimes committed by foreigners since I had already been sentenced.

Somebody had stolen a TV out of a shop in Wan Chai the previous year, so the police wanted to question me about it. I thought I knew who did it -- sounded like him -- but it wasn't me. So, I was taken back to the classrooms.

I was with a bunch of remand prisoners who the police visit quite regularly so we went through the dining hall first so that they could be dropped off. I was then led to the back door of the hall and stepped out into the small courtyard there ... right into the path of the Cat A's coming down the stairs.

I had studied him for months: his height; build and who he walked with. I had full knowledge of the time and the location, who he walked with, and where he was always placed in the group.

I was on him before anyone could have realised their mistake. He fell back onto the stairs, I had scattered everyone in front of him and he fell hard on his back, his head hitting the stone stairs behind him. I grabbed the front of his shirt, picked him up and hit him backwards, again his head making a great noise as it hit the stairs like a boiled egg being cracked.

I fell forwards and my knee went into his stomach, just missing his balls where I was aiming. All I saw was him; all I heard was my breathing. I saw his teeth, those teeth that had marked skin in his crime against two innocent, defenceless kids. I punched those teeth, once, twice, and then I was in the air, falling upwards away from him. I spun around and was at the bottom of the stairs, I wasn't looking at him anymore, but I only saw his face. I had done it; satisfaction overwhelmed me, drowning out the sensation of batons raining down on me.

Unable to feel the weight of the officers on top of me, unable to hear anything apart from the joy of achieving a goal, taking control, completing a task, and getting some of our own back against a guy who had destroyed so much.

There was a buzz amongst the officers. At first, I was dragged to the governor's office where everyone was taken when there was a fight but instead of waiting there for hours before finally being seen by him and given my sentence, I was dragged off straight away to solitary.

I was thrown into a dark cell and the door slammed shut. I lay on the floor for ages, not wanting to move until I could tell that there were no officers around. It was then that my senses started awakening and the pain from the beating I had taken started to fill every part of me. I was sick, soiled myself and wet myself. I could not get off the floor; I was so weak.

I don't remember how long I lay there, but the unmistakable noise of many boots came down the corridor and my cell door was opened again. They swarmed in and all started taking their best shots at me. I crawled into a ball trying to protect myself, but they pulled my legs one way and my arms the other and let fly with their batons into my stomach.

They were all screaming at me. I couldn't understand what they were saying but I had obviously pissed them off. They had made a mistake and were in the shit and the way they wanted payback was from my pain. They let me go and I crawled into a ball, tears and vomit flowing from my face. The door shut and I was left. I lay there for hours. I couldn't move. I was racked with pain; any movement sent waves of pain through all my other injuries. I eventually reached up and grabbed a blanket and covered myself, I lay there until the next day.

I dreamt. I dreamt of the two kids he and his friends had murdered. My dreams took me to that hillside and I watched them do it. I witnessed the whole event in my mind. As the event was happening, I looked into the kids' eyes, and they looked back at me. It was as if time and space had mingled. They knew what was happening; they knew what I was going to do and what I had done. We connected for a brief, fleeting moment and then I was back in my cell, on the ground, stinking, but at peace.

It's strange but that morning I didn't feel triumphant. Why would I? I was happy with what I had done but it didn't change anything. Yes, I had got what I felt was a bit of rightly deserved justice for those two kids, but my mind started to play tricks on me straight away. What if I had attacked the wrong guy? I only had acid boy's finger point to decide who out of a group of guys I would attack, who I believed was guilty of a heinous crime. But never mind, whoever I had attacked was a bad guy anyway. He wasn't in here for stealing someone's roses, was he?

Chapter Sixteen

By the end of January, I had hit a wall. I didn't know what had happened to me but, suddenly, my mental health took a huge nosedive. I was still going to Thingummy's every night but I tended to sit by myself and not talk to anyone.

This had been going on for about a week when, one night, a friend, Janine approached me. She seemed concerned and sat down next to me.

'Are you okay?' she asked.

Without thinking, I said, 'Fuck off'.

She sat there a moment and then told me that if I needed to talk, she was there for me.

A couple of days later, I had just got back from a field trip to the Supreme Court with my law class when I bumped into Melanie and Ricardo. Melanie gave me a huge hug and that was it, I was back.

That weekend, I hung out with Matt and Andy. We got so super pissed that we ended up wandering around down by the harbour and stumbled across the Peak bus. The bus was one of those open-top double-deckers that tourists got to travel up to the Peak.

The three of us must have had the exact same thought at the same time as we all climbed up the back of the bus, onto the top deck. As Andy had passed his driving test earlier that month, he took the driver's seat, I don't know how but he found the keys, started the bus up and drove it around the car park whilst Matt and I rolled around on the back seat. He just as quickly parked it again and we all ran up the stairs and climbed down the back.

The next weekend was my first proper house party. It was Zoe's birthday party. I knew her from the In Place, a gorgeous Irish lassie, who took no shit and had a diamond character. I liked her, she was awesome.

She went to South Island school along with a few other people I knew including members of a local band called Suicide Alley. I'd heard of them; Matt had told me that they had named themselves after the alley behind the In Place where people had died from drugs overdoses.

It had all the makings of a great party.

I met with a couple of friends in Thingummy's then we all jumped in a taxi and headed up towards Zoe's flat in Mid-Levels. It was jumping when we got there, you could hear the music from the street as soon as the taxi pulled up. It wasn't a big apartment and the band had set up using the balcony and part of the living room. We got there just at the right time as they had just started.

They played a brilliant set of all the music that I loved, all rock music, some modern and some from the late 60s and 70s. For a school band, they were excellent.

After they had finished, the drinking continued and I was aware that other things were being taken as well. Someone was so out of it that they walked straight through a glass door.

Eventually, those of us who were left fell asleep in different places. I slept in the living room with a girl I had met that night along with about ten others.

In the morning, we were woken by Lloyd, the bass player for the band playing the opening bars of Patience by Guns N' Roses whilst sitting on the balcony with the early morning sun behind him. It was almost spiritual.

That night, it was Chinese New Year and so we all went up the Peak to watch the fireworks. That's when I also met Anna, who is Ricardo's sister, again. We ended up getting off with each other. I'd never even kissed one girl as many times as I had kissed different girls in the time I'd been here. It was crazy, and I simply couldn't stop myself even though I was still supposedly going out with Allison. That had been confirmed the week before at the In Place, but I was like a kid in a sweetie store.

This place was so crazy that I was with a different girl every week.

Well, let's be honest, it was more like three different girls each week.

第十七章

Solitary is rough. They give prisoners as little contact with others as possible. My clothes were in a mess, but they never came to give me a change. Late into the first full day, I managed to get myself off the floor and onto the hard fibreglass bed. It wasn't any more comfortable than the floor but it did give me a little insulation from the cold, hard concrete.

My food would come, late, cold, meagre and almost inedible, served without a smile. That night was bad. My body was trying to heal but every time I moved, I hurt. It reminded me of the physical pain of withdrawal. Every nerve that had been injured screamed when any pressure was applied to it.

The next morning, I managed to get up. I stumbled to the small sink at the back of the cell to check to see if there was water because sometimes there wasn't. This time, I was lucky. I took off my soiled clothes very slowly trying not to retch at the stink because each time I did my ribs would ache.

I washed my clothes as well as I could and looped them around the bars at the front of the cell to try and get as much water out of them as possible. I swung them around my head after that to try to dry them. It was cold in the cell; the only source of heat came from the very dim light bulb in the ceiling.

Eventually, I just had to put my clothes back on. I couldn't heat myself the usual way by exercising because my body was now starting to seize up. That night, I was cold and damp. I started to shiver and that helped my pain a bit. It was like giving my bruised body a little massage.

Every day, I would get up expecting to be taken out of the cell to the governor's office to get sentenced for my crime of assault, but no one would ever come apart to throw me some food now and again.

Each day, I lay there in the near dark, listening to the sounds of the prison but seeing nothing of it. I was supposed to get out for an hour each day for exercise but when I suggested it to a guard he just laughed. So, I just lay there thinking. My thoughts were of hopelessness. I didn't regret what I had done in the fight, but I regretted being here in the first place.

I began to think through my whole life, recounting all the sadness that I had survived … all the feelings of loneliness, self-hatred, fear and loathing. I cried a lot. I thought of my family. How I felt that they all hated me, and quite rightly so. I thought of friends and how I had let them all down.

I felt sometimes that the best way to go would be just to kill someone and then spend the rest of my life in solitary, slowly going insane like an animal trapped in a too-small cage. I would stare out of the cell, trying to make out shapes beyond the barred windows of the hallway. It looked out onto a wall. I would count the bricks; and start making shapes with my mind. One day I lay there trying to contact people I knew through thoughts alone. I thought that I would be able to use the power of my brain to contact them and that they would hear me and say hello back.

I spent hours doing that, then days, with no one answering. I believed that I was going to be in here forever. Maybe there was some prison rule that I hadn't been told about that would cause me to take over someone else's sentence -- he was to go free and I was to be in here for life.

I was slowly going crazy but didn't realise it. When people go crazy, it doesn't occur to them that they have, it just becomes their everyday normal. I thought back to the time when it was evident I had lost my mind, just before prison.

I was sitting on the steps of a building in Causeway Bay pretending to be in a music video. I was singing my favourite songs whilst being filmed by a secret film crew. People would be walking past staring at me as I would very animatedly sing to an invisible camera. At the time I thought it was brilliant. What a great video, all these unsuspecting people not knowing that they were in a music video of a famous Western singer. But I was just a crazy guy sitting on the steps singing to myself in the middle of the day.

Weeks passed until one day they let me out. I was taken to reception where I was given new clothes and then taken to the dining hall. My eyes burned with the sunlight. I had no idea what time of day it was. When I got into the hall, it was full of my group of prisoners. I was glad to be with them again. I got my food and sat at a separate table. I ate and then was taken out of the hall first by myself.

Everyone was staring at me. I even thought I got a couple of smiles, but I don't know. I was taken back to my cell where all my belongings were. I made my bed, lay down and cried.

When I heard the other prisoners coming, I got up, picked up a book and sat on my bed. This time they just walked past -- no spitting and no name-calling. They just stared at me. Nothing was mentioned about the fight by anyone. But the Cat As never walked past our classroom again. We never really saw them again, only at a distance when they were in their exercise yard.

Chapter Seventeen

It was Friday night. It must have been some kind of holiday because everywhere was jumping. I had been in Thingummy's all night and was now standing on the street outside with a large group of friends. We were all in a heated discussion about where we were going to head next. All of us were a bit pissed and standing in the middle of the streets holding pints.

There were groups of teenagers all over the street. Some sitting on the steps on the pavement, others in the middle of the road. I spotted another three that I knew from either the year below me or maybe it was two years below me, I couldn't remember.

They caught my attention because they kept looking up towards us whilst they were whispering. They were planning something, I didn't know what, but I was on guard instinctively. I may have had no problems here in Hong Kong but that didn't change who I was after years of being attacked and beaten in Scotland, I was always on edge.

What are they up to, I wondered as I tried not to be obvious that I had seen them looking at us. I turned back to my group of friends and joined the conversation.

We were back to discussing which club to go to when there was a pull on my sleeve.

I looked around and then down to the girl who had been with the two other guys who were whispering.

'Do you know where we can buy some grass?'

She said with a big bright smile.

Firstly, I had never seen grass.

Secondly, I had no idea where to buy it.

Thirdly, I wanted to look cool as she had come up to me to ask, so I didn't want to admit that I didn't know.

Fourthly, I didn't think that they should be taking drugs.

They looked drunk already. It had only been quite recently that I'd had to look after a young girl who was so drunk, she was unconscious. She was lying on the street outside Thingummy's, dumped by her pals in a short blue dress with drunk old Mr Lee trying to pull up her dress. She was going to be raped, no doubt about it.

I picked her up and took her to the park across the road and put her on a bench. I sat with her that night for five hours until she sobered up enough to go home.

So, I thought for a moment.

'Wait here', I said.

I headed up into the same park, where I had sat with Lucy that night when she was unconscious. I took out three Marlboro lights from the packet I had and then removed the film sleeve from the packet. I open the three cigarettes and put the tobacco into the sleeve. I held it up to the dim light that illuminated the park into hundreds of shadows. I was totally in the dark about whether it looked anything like grass. But I shrugged my shoulders to myself and headed back out onto the street and nodded for the three kids to come over.

'20 bucks'

They handed me the money and I handed them the 'drugs'.

'Be careful, it's really strong', I said.

They nodded and scurried away towards the 7-Eleven to get rolling papers. I went back over to my friends and joined back in with the drunken discussion.

'Where do you want to go?'

'I don't mind'.

'Where do you want to go?'

'I told you I don't mind'.

We decided eventually to go and get something to eat before we went up to Lan Kwai Fong. We were all drunk so thought 7-Eleven noodles would help us last the night; I used the $20 that she had given me to put towards our noodle bill.

An hour later, we were back outside Thingummy's at the same spot waiting for a few others to come up from the cave below. When they climbed out of the darkness and joined us, we all turned and headed towards clubland. To my right, I saw the three kids from earlier. The two boys were sitting on the pavement rolling around whilst the girl who had taken the 'drugs' off me was swinging around a lamppost, head flung back.

When she saw me and managed to focus her eyes, she said

'That was good shit man, thanks a lot'.

I nodded to her, trying to hold myself together, as soon as my group walked around the corner I started laughing,

'What's your fuckin' problem man?'

I told them what had happened, and everyone started laughing.

I kept laughing at the three kids stoned from three Marlboro lights without a filter as we headed toward the noise and the lights, clubland, for a night of full-on dancing. I had no idea then how much that one interaction was going to devastate my life.

I was still going to school, but it was becoming less and less frequent. I had completely given up going to law classes and concentrated only on all the classes that completed the business course.

My Saturdays were usually spent taking part in some sort of school activity. One was spent painting our house room, Rutherford, green. On a few others, I went with a group to a local Vietnamese boat people detention centre and played table tennis with the kids.

And one was spent washing and waxing Mr Harding's car. That was my first and only Saturday detention which was the most serious detention you could get at Island School. Melanie, Dom and I were caught smoking on the school roof one day by Mr Harding, our housemaster, so we were all made to do a detention one Saturday morning. I volunteered to wash his car for him whilst everyone else had to sit in a classroom and write some essay he had come up with. It wasn't quite the Breakfast Club.

Not long after that, we had the school athletics meet, with a little more style and pizazz than what I had experienced in Scotland. The school hired out a huge athletics stadium down by the waterfront in Wan Chai, a full-on athletics stadium. It was awesome.

I was not taking part in anything due to my newfound behaviour. Back in Glasgow, I would have entered lots of different races and events, not in the hope of winning but just because I enjoyed it. It was something you did really by yourself, something you could use to help with stress and anxiety. Moving to Hong Kong, I now used alcohol for this purpose, like most of the other students I knew.

This really was fascinating, the percentage of students that drank, underage, in weird drinking dens was incredibly high. Even the good students could be seen out and about every so often getting pissed. Surely, we all stank of stale booze first thing in the morning at registration, but then maybe those teachers had been out the night before as well?

If the school held a competition for the most drunk kid and the craziest nightlife, rather than athletics, then I feel I would be up there with the best of them.

Whose responsibility was it anyway?

The school?

The parents?

Ours?

More than once, I had to escort one of my female friends to the special chemist in Wan Chai to support them as they bought the morning after pill after having sex with some unknown guy.

That was a great chemist. Questions were never asked. I went there one day with a friend as I had a cough that was probably brought on by the sub-tropical climate and air pollution. I was given this pink cough mixture that we both got a little high off.

The next two weeks consisted of the usual partying, more girls and then sobering up at the athletics track. Cheering when we were supposed to and sleeping the rest of the time.

I was seeing more of Anna now, even though I was still going out with Allison. But Allison rarely came out and I always felt better with company. I enjoyed being shown affection by someone. I'd never had it before and, for the first time, my self-esteem had risen from below sea level.

She was incredibly hot, Portuguese with olive skin and long brown hair. She just seemed to turn up everywhere I was. Okay maybe we both helped that to happen but sometimes it was just spontaneous, and it helped that she was the best kisser I had ever met.

Unfortunately, her ex, John, wasn't very pleased with our behaviour and so he decided to tell Allison about our affair one day at the athletics. She was crying for ages. I felt bad, I did. But we hardly saw each other anymore.

Anna and I spent the whole of that weekend together as I was due to start a week of work experience the following week so would not be going out at all.

I was going to be working as an office assistant at the English Schools Foundation or the ESF's head office. They ran all the foreign schools in Hong Kong, well most of them anyway. Luckily my dad was away working again so I'd be able to get to the couch early every night and would be okay in the morning. It was going to be the longest dry spell I'd had in six months; my body was in for a treat!

As I was getting ready early on Monday morning, I was feeling relaxed compared to my school friends. We had been discussing our work experience week coming up and a lot of them were completely stressed out. Strange, as most of them were going to be working at the company which their parents owned or where one of them was the CEO. Debbie was going to work at the Hilton Hotel, which was where she lived because her dad was the hotel manager!

I had asked my dad a few weeks beforehand, and he simply said no. Of course he did, pointless even to consider it. I could have asked Peter at Thingummy's if I could work there for a week. Just like Debbie, I would be working where I was living!

But as I couldn't find anywhere, I was made to work at the ESF's head office. I wasn't worried, it wasn't as if I hadn't worked before. Running my own car washing business at 12, working at the Coral Reef aquarium shop at 14 and then the Navy, it wasn't the first time that I had joined the rat race.

I'd even completed work experience at school in Glasgow when I worked with the porters for a week delivering both live and dead bodies to different departments at the Victoria Royal Infirmary. I still remember my first wrap and tag cadaver, Karen, who I had to collect and deliver by myself to the weird people in the morgue and help to pick up and slide into the freezer.

That was the week before I went to join my dad on an oil tanker in Houston when I was 15, the trip I lost my virginity to a Venezuelan prostitute.

第18章

Something had changed in my mind. Actually, not just in my mind. I could feel the change in my whole body, in every cell. The cells fizzed with this new sensation. I was going to fight back.

I had finally lost my mind, but I didn't realise it. I was not going to sit there and be attacked; I was going to attack first. I wasn't quite hearing voices -- well I don't think so -- but I kept telling myself:

'Attack! Attack! No more Mr Nice Guy. I'm going to die here but I'm taking everyone with me!'

I would get up early, before the radio, and work out. I had to be strong when the time came. I would dream of all the scenarios of how I was going to do it, where I was going to do it, and what the outcome would be. I would find myself dying repeatedly in my dreams. Smiling, looking upwards, and shouting out:

'Sorry, mum'.

In my dreams, there would be bodies all around me, blood in pools around the lifeless bodies of the prisoners I had taken with me. Officers in the distance would run towards me, in slow motion, with truncheons held high.

I could feel the life slowly leaving me; it would be peaceful, almost tranquil. This was me preparing to die, to be at peace. I dreamt about how people would react to the news. People from my past aghast at the brutality I had inflicted on people.

After finishing my work out, I would shower and clean my cell. Sometimes I would have to sit for what seemed like an hour before the radio even came on. The night officer would sometimes go past and tell me to go back to bed because it was only 4.00 am. But I wouldn't. I would continue with my plan. I had the look of the mad. I would stare at everyone with this look of pure evil in my eyes. I could see them stop and take a second look, then they appeared to take a step back from me as I was exuding such evil and malice.

As we were lined up outside each morning, I could hear the others whispering about me.

'Watch out Gwai Gi is crazy.'

'Gwai Gi will kill us.'

'We have to be safe.'

The voices in my head were like a thousand whispers, all mixed up.

I would growl at people if they looked at me. In the dining hall, I emitted a low growl while picking up my food and when I ate it. At my table, I would put my left hand around my food and drink, lower my head over my plate but with my head tilted up towards the others while I ate, like a snarling dog. They all just sat there staring at me.

In the workshop, I would pace up and down at one end and they would sit at the other, staring at me. I would be muttering to myself and they would be speaking in hushed tones. This happened in the classroom as well, although there I took a chair and put it with the back to the wall and faced everyone and the door. The Cat As didn't walk past anymore but I was watching for them.

Chapter 18

I was a little sad that my week of work experience at the head office of the English Schools Foundation was coming to an end. When I had first been told that that was where I was going to work, I wasn't happy. My new party lifestyle meant that I was concentrating less and less in school. I only found it possible to sleep at home when my dad wasn't there as that was when I could get some sort of sleep on the old sofa in the front room.

Even when he wasn't there, I had become so entrenched in my new life that I still went out drinking every night at Thingummy's. I would head home sometimes at midnight, but mostly at 3.00 am after the clubs closed. When he was at home, I stayed with friends, lots of different friends. Or I would stay out in the clubs as late as I could, sneak home and get changed then head out to school, sometimes without having slept at all.

Anyway, I had enjoyed this week. I had a list of things I had to do in the office each morning. The best was weighing and then stamping the mail in the franking machine. When I had finished, I took it all down to post at the General Post Office in Central. This gave me the freedom to walk around the amazing city streets, discovering back alleys and shortcuts.

The city continually excited me. I would see openings and head towards them to see where they led to. Some of the alleys were so narrow and disgusting that you had to go sideways very carefully so that you didn't touch the sides.

I would find entrances to underground caverns where the rain would gather so as not to flood the city. I would go through buildings and find so many of them connected above ground level that the walk from Wan Chai to Central could be done without ever having to go down to street level.

Whenever a security guard in a building would try and stop me, I would show them my red post bag and shout, 'Mail boy!' They would smile and wave me through. I had complete access to the city and started to dream that it was mine and always would be. I was part of its heartbeat, the hidden part that no-one could see. I ran through the veins to keep its massive organs fed. Without me, the city would fail.

When I eventually got back to the office, they would sometimes ask why it had taken me so long when the last boy they had only took a quarter of the time it took me. I just said that I was new here and kept getting lost, hoping that I wouldn't get into trouble from the school.

I was just getting the mail ready for the last time, my last journey with my little red bag, when I saw two of the staff from school walk into the office. 'Shit,' I thought, 'I'm busted, the fuckers have complained to the school about my postman adventures'.

They looked at me without smiling and went into a meeting room. I couldn't believe that I was going to get pulled up for this. My friends told me that they had been doing nothing all week whilst pretending to be working at their parents' offices, getting 5-star reviews whilst on the beach.

At first, I had been jealous of them but as the week went on and I had started to enjoy my 'job', I had got over it. Now I was pissed off with them. The lucky bastards. But then that's the law of the jungle, isn't it? If you can get away with it, then do it, just like I had been doing with the mail. So well done them, I wasn't going to say anything to save my skin. I had learnt that a long time ago. No point saying anything as it only got you into more bother and nobody ever believed me anyway.

I recognized the two staff members but hadn't had any interaction with them before, so maybe they weren't there to see me after all. Maybe I was being paranoid from the lack of sleep, food and the excessive amount of partying. And anyway, this was their head office; they could have been here for anything. I tried to regain my focus, get back to the franking machine and shake the negative, paranoid thoughts out of my head. Then I heard my name called.

'Can you come here please?'

Not really a request, more a demand. No matter, I put the letter down that I had just franked and walked over towards the meeting room, still trying to work out what I had done so wrong to get this sort of treatment from the school. I had always been here on time, never asked to leave early, completed all the tasks asked of me, okay, maybe a little slowly, but they had been completed. I walked in to be greeted by stern faces; I tried to muster a smile.

'Sit down, please.'

I sat and listened.

'We have information that you are a drug addict and a drug dealer. You are using hard drugs and selling hard drugs to students in the school.'

The floor opened up; I fell. I kept falling and there was nothing to stop me. I was spinning round and round, bouncing off every word that came out of their mouths like the sides of a deep cavern ripping my clothes and my skin, each word stinging my nerves as it came to me at maximum velocity.

'What?' I squeaked.

'There has been an investigation over the last few weeks based on information received that you are a drug dealer and have been selling drugs in school.'

I was in a brain coma, a vegetative state. I'm sure saliva was dripping from my open mouth and down my chin.

I had switched off and only heard a word here and there.

'He told us … has witnessed … you sold marijuana to …'

Boom! I was wide awake, sitting upright, with my pupils gaining control, my cognition coming back online.

'Wait', I said, 'I know what you're talking about. That wasn't drugs; that was cigarettes. It was a joke; I don't know where to buy drugs and I've never seen hard drugs.'

Then there came a list of names.

'Do you know such and such? They said that you did this and that. Tell us about such and such.'

These were my friends they were talking about. They were saying that these friends of mine had said all this about me. I couldn't believe it. But then again, I could. Had they said all these things to save themselves? Rule of the jungle … last one in, first one out.

And then they said, 'We've had calls from concerned parents.'

I tried to work out what a concerned parent was, I tried to think of going home and telling my 'concerned' parents about things happening at school. Then I thought of kids going home and getting into trouble for something and then trying to get themselves off the hook by saying:

'The new guy sells drugs.'

I did know a dealer, a big guy called Rick, who I would see at the In Place sometimes and he would fill me with tales of going and purchasing big sausages worth of hash from China and selling it for a big profit. But as money orientated as I was, I was never interested in that kind of thing.

I had never seen a hard drug in my life, didn't know anyone who took them and, to be honest, would have difficulty in telling you what a hard drug was or what one even looked like. I was raised by alcoholics and that was my 'drug' of choice, along with cigarettes. I thought I was naughty drinking underage and getting caught once by Mr Harding smoking Marlboros on the school roof!

'Okay', they finished with, 'please collect all your items and come directly to the school and wait at the principal's office.'

With that, they were gone, and my work experience week was finished. What else was finished I had no idea, but it wouldn't be long until I found out.

第19章

'What the fuck are you all looking at?'
'Fuck off, the lot of you.'
'You want some, come and get it pricks'.
I picked up a table and threw it. A chair was next.
The rest of the class was huddled in a corner. The alarm started ringing. The officer was shouting at me trying to calm me down. Tears were streaming down my face. The voices in my head had finally formed into one maelstrom of thunder.

Everyone had been whispering about me and they were all taking little sideways looks at me. I had had enough. I jumped up and started screaming. The classroom door flew open, and five officers ran in and pinned me to the ground. Blows of feet, fists, knees and batons poured down on top of me. I was screaming; I shit myself, pissed myself, everything just released out of me. I was dragged out and down to the governor's office.

They finally got off me when I had calmed down. I managed to stop sobbing and pulled myself up and tried to stand as proud as I could be in my shit and piss-stained uniform.

The governor decided that because of all the aggravation, I was to be kept apart from the other prisoners. He refused my request to go to solitary. Every morning, I was to be taken out of my cell last and every night I was to be put in first.

That night, I was marched to the cells by myself and put into my cell before the others came upstairs. My cell was the first on the landing. The first prisoners to go past were the Vietnamese dogs. As they went past, they started hurling insults at me. I reacted and ran to the front of my cell where I was met with an onslaught of spit and fists flying. I went mental, screaming, and ripping off my shirt. I was clawing at the cell door wanting to rip it open so that I could grab one of them and beat them to death.

After they passed, the Chinese then walked past. They all stared at me and cursed at me, issuing obvious threats. I didn't run forward this time in case I was spat at again. I just concentrated on working out. Doing push-ups and sit-ups, trying to ignore their threats. It was like this every morning and every night for the next few weeks.

I tried my best to ignore it by turning my back and doing more push-ups and sit-ups. But every day I was becoming more and more mentally damaged. I was starting to lose it again.

At night, my dreams would be full of being murdered in the prison; the different ways it would happen. Sometimes I would go out in a blaze of glory; other times I would be set upon by a bunch of them and be stabbed more times than I could count and slowly die there on the ground staring up to the sky.

One Sunday, we were taken to the football pitch for the first time. This had been a moment I had been dreading ever since the trouble began. I remember the days at school playing football when, if someone didn't like you, they would kick you to pieces. This was what I was expecting to happen today. I was never any good at football. I was always chosen last at school or even after school when we played in the fields at the bottom of my street. I usually ended up playing in goal where I was quite good because of my size and my ability to save the ball from any angle. I don't know how; I just seemed to be able to judge it for some reason.

As the teams were being selected, I noticed that the big brother was talking to one of his lieutenants. I was put into the II [illegal immigrant] team and went into the goal. It was very clear from the starting whistle what was going to happen. The lieutenant that the big brother had been talking to was their best player. He had been given instructions not to score past me, but to get the ball near our goal where he was to kick the shit out of me every chance he had.

It really was schoolboy stuff and I was prepared. I had gone to school in Glasgow, and I was English, and everybody knew it. I was also very bad at socialising with people and was bullied continuously at school. Most of it was my own doing, according to my teachers and family. I had been attacked both on and off the football pitch all the way through primary school and secondary. It was nothing new to me.

From the very first kick of the ball, the lieutenant was given the ball and ran straight towards me. He had too many thoughts going through his head about how he was going to get me that as soon as he was close, I took the ball off him before he had time to decide. He ran back to the big brother who was not happy with him. Time and time again he came at me, from every angle, and every time I took the ball off him without him being able to touch me.

He was getting more and more frustrated. He began to even forget about the ball and just tried to get close enough to either kick or punch me but every time I managed to get the ball and even sometimes take him out whilst doing so. I would go down low, throw my body at him, knock him flying and stand up with the ball. By now the big brother was screaming at him and instead of being 11-a-side it was now just one against one and I was playing the game of my life. I was enjoying it. In fact, I loved it. I don't know who won or whether it was a draw, but I know that they never scored against us. As the final whistle blew, they were defeated. They looked defeated and were walking defeated.

As we were leaving the pitch and I had my chest pumped up, the big brother walked over to me and said, 'This is China' and walked off. I knew what he meant. But for the first time, I realised that this bunch of supposedly fierce prisoners were nothing more than a bunch of bullies, school dropouts who feared the guards and had to come up with pathetic attempts to get me instead of just an all-out assault which would get them into trouble.

I wouldn't find out until much later that that wasn't the case. I was being protected by forces unknown to me at that point and that any attack on me had to be sanctioned by someone a lot further up.

The next week, we went out to play again. This time I wasn't in goal and I was chosen to be on the same side as the big brother and his lieutenant. Maybe winning a football game was more important to them as we played well together. Maybe this would be the turning point I had dreamed of.

I played a fantastic pass from the right wing. It curled into the box right on the end of the lieutenant's foot and he drove the ball into the net. I turned around and jogged away knowing that no one would come up to congratulate me.

In the second half, the game continued from where it had left off with me playing on the wing and crossing the ball over to the lieutenant for him to score. I was running down the left wing after a ball, totally relaxed now, not looking out to see if anyone was going to attack me when it happened. They had played a good hand.

I was relaxed. I was concentrating on the game and the ball when a tall guy came thundering into me. He took me mid-leg with both his feet. He went straight through me. I went flying and skidded along the ground for a few feet before I came to a stop.

The adrenalin was pumping through me, and I jumped up straight away ready for any afters. But then I fell. I didn't understand what was going on. I tried to get up again but fell straight back down. I then felt hands on my shoulders pushing me back down onto the ground; it was one of the guards. I stared at them over my shoulders and then looked at the others as they started to come around me. I then looked down and the bottom half of my leg was all wrong. The rest is a bit hazy.

I was taken to the prison hospital and a short time later I was in an ambulance being driven out of the prison. I don't know if they had given me any pain relief, but my head was swimming. I can't remember how long it took but we eventually arrived at the hospital where I was wheeled into the reception. I was handcuffed to the trolley to make sure I couldn't jump up and run away.

I was a bit out of it but remember looking at all the people around me in the waiting room saying things like 'crazy foreigner'. I was making some strange noises. I was then taken to a lift where I saw some frightened-looking people, probably because of me, a foreigner making strange faces and noises whilst handcuffed to a bed and surrounded by prison guards with lots of guns.

We eventually got to the prison ward which was in the basement of the hospital where I was wheeled to a large cell that had eight hospital beds behind a wall of bars. I was taken in and dumped in one of the beds. I then fell asleep.

Chapter 19

I got to the school at noon and waited at the principal's office as directed. I was called into his office at 12.15 pm and, by 12.20 pm, I had been expelled and told to go and collect my belongings from my locker.

I had been given a letter asking my parents to come to a meeting on Monday and that was that. Instead of going to get my things, I went out the hole in the fence next to one of the basketball courts near the back stairs. This was my smoking area of choice after Mr Harding caught us on the roof. I sat there in the woods smoking cigarettes, one after another, trying to formulate what happened to me. It had all happened so quickly.

They hadn't listened to a word I had said, they had already made up their mind. They believed everyone else and not me. Why? It didn't seem fair. How can that happen? What was the point of coming to ask me anything when they weren't going to listen or even check on anything I said?

If they had spoken to the kids who I had sold the 'grass' to as well as the friends who were there that night and who I had told about the deal, well, surely, they would have had to apologise to me and admit that were wrong. And who were the people who said I was a drug addict? What drugs had I taken? What proof did they have?

They didn't have any. They just decided to hang me out to dry because one of those kids had got caught doing something, so they had told their whole story. And wait a minute, weren't those kids getting expelled as well? They bought what they thought were drugs. But no, I was the big bad drug pusher when all I had done was try and stop three kids taking drugs. I didn't like drugs. I wasn't a drug user and never would be. I drank. That's what I did, and I liked it.

'I wish I could have a drink right now,' I thought to myself whilst grinding out my last cigarette.

I went to my locker in the Einstein sixth form room. I told those who were there that I had been kicked out.

'What?'

'Why?'

'No way?'

I collected my things and walked down to the ground floor. I saw Allison there, my girlfriend at the time. She had a look of concern on her face. She ran up to me and threw her arms around me,

'They've expelled me,' I whispered in her ear, that's when the tears came.

Others started to gather around us standing there, friends coming to see what was wrong. The secret was out and being passed around. Kind words were being used towards me, with tears from close friends, the grief of teenagers for a downed friend.

But then I noticed others not coming to me. I saw those whose names had been mentioned to me in that meeting room; the names were looking at me sideways as they walked out of school. They didn't come up to me, they walked past me. The looks they gave me were new to me in Hong Kong but so, so familiar from my school days in Glasgow.

I couldn't quite understand the emotion they were displaying but that look was familiar. Generally, bad things happened after I saw that look … isolation, fear, depression. The look I couldn't work out but, in the aftermath, I could. Those feelings slowly took over the grief that I was feeling, loss taken over by uneasiness. A feeling that I had forgotten for so long in this teenage paradise. A feeling that came with terrible memories and terrible ramifications. I walked with friends down to McDonald's, trying to make sense of what was happening.

'There's a drug bust every year', someone said.

'Remember? It was [such and such] last year,' someone else said.

'But I don't do drugs or sell them', I explained.

'Someone thinks you do.'

So, was that it. For the importance of the school -- to keep on the good side of its powerful parents -- they had to be seen as taking a hard stance and this year I was the scapegoat. I could understand this logically. It wasn't fair, it wasn't right, and it wasn't fucking true.

What felt even worse was knowing that no one was coming to my defence, yet again. I'd had lies told about me before, like the time I allegedly beat up three lads at the golf course in Glasgow and got suspended. Even though I had a witness who saw that I was the one being beaten, and I had the bruises to prove it, I was still blamed.

But this hurt even more. It hurt because it was an untruth which affected my friends. I could handle taking the fall for something but when someone attacked my friends, it got me angry. I would always defend my friends no matter if they were in the wrong or not. I was loyal like a dog in that way.

Many of the others had also been interviewed at the school during the week. They had been told that I had given the teachers their names. I was the grass; I was the informant. But that was just simply impossible. I was the last to be interviewed, the last to be spoken to. How could

I possibly have given all their names? Forget the fact that I wouldn't have done that, as that was just my word against the teachers.

But the simple fact of timing would surely stand up in any court. They had come to me last and said that all my friends had given my name. They had spoken to my friends before me and said that I had given their names. It was just not possible. And there you have it; it was a setup. My name wasn't the only one mentioned, but I was the only one getting expelled. I was both the executioner and the executed.

My paradise was crumbling right in front of my eyes. I stumbled out of McDonald's and onto the busy streets. I didn't see my city anymore. I was on autopilot. I walked the long walk home, instead of getting the bus. I didn't want to be near anyone. I resolved on that walk to go to the In Place that night. It was Friday night. What else would I do? Sit at home after giving Mum the letter and watch her drink herself into oblivion whilst watching shit on TV waiting for whatever the 9.30 pm movie was going to be, on either ATV World or TVB Pearl, the two English channels.

I got in the house, handed my mum the letter and told her my side of my story as briefly as I could. She got some whisky to calm her nerves, nearly downed it in one and just said, 'I'm glad your father is away'. That was it.

I had a shower and got changed. It was early but I decided to go straight out. I would again walk down to Central to get the MTR to the In Place. I went out the back door, crunching through the thousands of cockroaches, smoking many cigarettes.

I took a different route from the normal one, trying to take as much time as possible before I got to the MTR. My thoughts during that walk turned to despair. The feelings that I had left behind, what felt like years ago but was only months ago. Loneliness engulfed me. Only yesterday, I had a beautiful girlfriend and a huge group of friends who were always there for me in person or on the phone. Now I was a dirty drug dealer who had been expelled from school, the lowest of the low. All of what I had built up around me was lying in shreds, scattered at my feet, crunched like the cockroaches and just like the photos that fell out of an envelope sent to my mum years ago.

I remember that day clearly. I must have been about 10 years old and my mum and I had just returned from a lovely day out together. We had been on a long bus trip. This was one of only a handful of days when our mother-and-son relationship had any joy in it.

As we got home, my mum opened the sliding door to the front porch. There was some post that had been delivered whilst we were out. She bent down and picked it up. On the top, there was a brown envelope. She opened this one first and out poured ripped family photographs, onto the floor. They were ripped into small pieces, but you could still make out the faces of our family in the pieces. Along with the photos came a note from my dad's mum, my grandmother,

'You have ruined our family.'

That was just how I felt right at that moment. But the note was my conscience and the photos were my friends.

'I need a drink to steady my nerves.'

It was 9.00 am and we were due at the school at 10.00 am. It wasn't just 'a' drink; my mum managed to down a couple of large whiskies before the taxi arrived to take us to the school. So, with her nerves settled, we drove up and down the hills to get the meeting.

The meeting was held in the principal's office. It didn't take long. After presenting their evidence, which I didn't bother to try and explain away as I could see no point whatsoever, I was officially expelled. Of course, my mum didn't try to slur anything in my defence. The only time I said anything was when Mr Harding comically asked:

'What would happen if we had those cigarettes scientifically studied to see what was inside?'

'You'd probably find tobacco', I said with a slight sneer.

They gave me a choice. I could either leave the school voluntarily which meant I could still sit my exams in May or they would call the police and ask them to investigate.

'Investigate what', I thought to myself. Anyway, that would mean my friends probably getting into trouble so I said I would just leave. I wanted to try to save what was left of my social circle and having the police involved would ruin everything. The police would find nothing on me. But then again, how could I prove that it was only tobacco I sold those kids that night?

'I'll leave', I said.

So, I left.

I put drunken mum in a taxi outside the school and went for a walk. I wandered the streets for hours. Whenever I had a question to answer, or a plan to make, I always walked. And I would walk for hours and hours, not stopping, even when hungry, thirsty, or just plain exhausted. I would keep on walking. My dad would be home next week, so I had seven days. Seven days to ... to do what? I didn't know. I couldn't figure it out. So, I continued walking.

I walked for about six hours that day, from Central to the West and then back to the east end of the island. The final walk uphill to my home was torture. I ached all over, internally and externally. As I fell on the sofa, my mum, now completely drunk and with tears still flowing, she wailed:

'What are you going to do?'
'What am I going to tell your dad?'
Ever so caring.
'Get a job,' I replied.
So, I did.

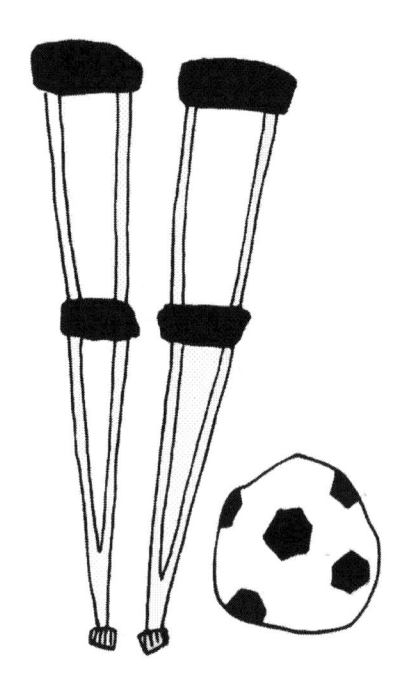

第20章

    I don't know how long I was asleep but when I woke up, I was dazed and confused. It was then that the pain hit me. My leg was bandaged from the groin to the ankle with a huge bandage and it was agony.

    As I looked around the room, little did I know that this would be my home for the next two months as I waited for an operation that would be cancelled constantly because someone who was not a convicted criminal needed an operation. It would also be the last time that I would ever take heroin, but that was all to come.

The first few days, I was off my head on pain relievers so I didn't take much in. Eventually, on the third day, I became fully conscious.

There were six beds in my room and they were all full. The guy next to me was an older guy who had tried to kill himself when he was arrested. He had murdered his wife and then taken the knife to himself. He had stabbed himself in the stomach and, when that hadn't worked, had tried to cut his throat. Looking at the wound, he very nearly succeeded. It was quite grotesque and would open a little sometimes if he laughed or coughed.

Two of the other guys just lay there and stared into space, dying of some sort of disease, I never did find out what it was. But they looked like they were about to die. They both did a short time later and were taken out without much fanfare. They were immediately replaced by another two who looked like they were also at the end of their life, but at least the sheets were still warm for them as they had not been changed.

All three meals a day were so much better than the prison food. They arrived in polystyrene pots and were just like the street food I used to buy at the little roadside cafés. They were generally delicious.

On the third day, I tried to get out of bed because I wanted a shower but when I tried, I just fell on the floor, pain shooting through my leg and then the rest of my body. I didn't know what was wrong with me and would never find out. I mean I know there was something wrong with my leg, but was the bone broken, ligaments torn, joint dislocated? I had no idea and nobody was about to tell me.

On day four, I eventually worked out how to operate my bed and managed to sit up properly. I was then able to see that there was another cell opposite us. Straight away, I witnessed a very strange complaint. An old guy was standing at the bars in his underwear with what could only be called one gigantic testicle hanging down through his shorts!

It was hard not to stare at such a sight. Strange songs started popping into my head to the same tune as 'Hitler only had one ball', but it was huge!

A short time later, a new patient was hauled into our cell and plonked on a rattan mat on the floor. After quite a long attempt at communicating, as he was an II from the north of China so he spoke Mandarin rather than Cantonese, we found out that he had woken up in the morning unable to feel anything below his waist; he was paralysed. But he also had twelve fingers and twelve toes which was just as interesting. He just lay there on the floor.

A short time later, someone in a white coat came in. I would have called him a doctor in any other hospital-related drama, but I really couldn't be sure. He spent the next thirty minutes with a needle torturing this guy on the floor by pushing the needle into lots of different parts of his body to see if he was acting or not. The poor guy had wee pools of blood all over his legs but also on his arms and body because they wanted to make sure that he registered pain in other places.

They started shouting at him for wasting their time and said that they would just throw him back into prison because they didn't believe him. They let him slump to the floor again and walked out. The wee guy's expression never changed. I don't know if his paralysis was psychological, but he appeared to be paralysed to me. He just lay there for days and then one day they came in and carted him off to who knows where.

After about a week of being confined to my bed, I finally saw someone who appeared to be employed in the medical profession. Three people in white coats came in and unwrapped my bandages. They poked me, bandaged me back up again and went out. The next thing I knew, I was being told to come to the cell door.

'Okay' I thought, 'I am going to do this.'

I had pissed in a bottle all week but that day I was going to get out of bed.

The most difficult and painful part was putting my leg lower than the rest of my body. When the blood flowed down into my leg, it caused so much pressure that the pain was almost too much. But this time I was prepared and managed to get my leg down and put the pain out of my head.

I hopped and slithered over to the cell door where I was told to put my hands through and they were handcuffed together, obviously to stop me from sprinting away! The cell door opened, and I was ushered out to the middle of the room outside the cells where a man in a white coat was standing with a cannula. I knew what it was; it wasn't my first time in hospital.

I felt quite excited. I was going to be operated on at last and have my leg fixed. I hobbled over to the white coat who had everything laid out on a hospital cabinet. He took my right hand and started to insert the needle of the cannula. In it went, and back out it came. In it went again and back out it came.

Where's the vein hiding, I thought trying not to show any pain on my face. Even then, I didn't want to show any negative emotion, not wanting to show any weakness. So, there I stood on my -- I don't know how smashed up -- leg with a white coat sticking a needle into the back of my right-hand time and time again, trying to get a vein.

The back of my hand was a bloody mess with bruising adding to the horrid discolouration. He gave up with that hand and started on the left, thankfully after only five or six attempts, he managed to find a vein and successfully inserted the cannula. He looked at me with beads of sweat on his brow and I stared right back at him. He honestly looked as if he expected me to kill him. But I just turned around and hobbled back to the cell door which was opened, back to my bed.

I only sat on the side of the bed and then asked to go to the toilet. I was vertical for the first time in a long time so what was the point in wasting that effort? I went to the bathroom and found it to be clean with a row of showers. Behind a separate door, I found, to my great delight, a bathtub. Oh my god, I was going to have a bath as soon as these bandages came off.

I went to the toilet and decided to have a half shower as well, as I was filthy. It wasn't the best as I had to keep my bandages clean, but it felt good. By the time I got back to the cell and had the cuffs taken off again, another white coat came in and stuck a needle in the cannula.

This guy told me that he was giving me a pre-op. At last, I was going to get fixed. Within the next hour, the op was cancelled. This happened so many times that I never got excited again. However, after about a month, the day finally came when I was given the pre-op and 30 minutes later, they came for me. I was handcuffed to a trolley and taken up to the theatre.

I was back in my bed when I came to, leg bandaged again but this time with a completely different feeling and not covered in blood.

I fell back to sleep.

Chapter 20

In less than a week, I was working in an estate agency in Wan Chai called Connell and Chan that was run by a middle-aged Scottish woman. I had been employed on the spot. I was a messenger. The pay was good and I got to spend most of my time out and about delivering things like contracts and other documents. I also was responsible for the post. So off I would go, discovering more and more of the fascinating city.

I found myself in some of the most amazing places. One day I was given an envelope to hand deliver to a chef at the Mandarin Oriental in Central. This was one of the poshest hotels around. I was slightly worried as me and Blakey had sometimes sneaked into the ground floor toilets and stole some of the aftershaves!! When I walked through the main door, I was worried that someone would recognise me and chase me out. But no, I was safe.

I had to ask where the kitchen was so I could deliver the letter. I walked up to reception and looked at the letter for the first time and started to laugh. This had to be a joke. I looked at the receptionist then back at the letter, and said in a clear voice:

'I have to hand-deliver this to Mr Munch, the head chef.'

I waited to be thrown out and was utterly surprised to be pointed in the direction of the kitchen, I headed off in the direction I was proffered. Having never been in one of these kitchens before, I was blown away. It wasn't a kitchen but a full-sized factory for food. It was massive with people pushing huge carts around with an assortment of wondrous goodies.

As it was around 10.00 am, these goodies were the elevenses', I thought to myself. Right in the middle of this food manufacturing empire was the head office of everything fine. A big box room was stuck in the middle of everything. I headed towards it, climbed the three small steps to the door and knocked politely. I waited and knocked again this time a little louder as there was a lot of background noise. There was no answer and, not knowing what else to do, I decided to try the handle. The door opened and I stepped into what looked like the captain's table on an old sailing ship. A big oval wooden table with the finest cutlery, plates and glassware I had ever seen. This must be where all the goodies were tasted.

Just then a man came in, Mr Munch himself. I handed him his letter and left quickly, just in case I shouldn't have let myself into his shrine.

Walking back to the office, I bumped into Angus, a Scottish guy that I'd met a couple of times previously. He told me he worked nearby and suggested we go for lunch sometime. So, I took his numbers, home and office, and said that I'd call him.

Back in the office, everyone was gathered around reading the South China Morning Post. A young Australian guy had just been given a three-year sentence for killing a guy. He said he had been drugged and woke up to find the guy molesting him. He smashed a bronze horse statue over his head. He only got three years! It shows you what an expensive lawyer can do for you.

第21章

The next day, I was asleep and woke to find a doctor -- yes, an actual doctor -- next to me talking to someone else with a white coat, but then he was off. I nearly found out what they did to me but not quite.

Over the next couple of days, I managed to get out of bed more often. I even managed to get a shower or two without getting my bandages too wet. One night, as I was lying on my bed, something very interesting happened.

One of the older prisoners was at the front cell bars keeping watch whilst another was calling up a tiny gap between the wall and the ceiling. He was shouting out instructions to someone above. Then after a minute or two, a small package started to appear and slowly came down towards the guy's outstretched hand. He managed to grab it, and the string disappeared again only to reappear with another package. This happened four or five more times. Then it was over, all packages were received. They quickly undid the packages. There were cigarettes and small wraps. When they opened them, I saw straight away that it was smack, heroin.

The instant that I saw it, I wanted it. After all these months spending hours alone in my prison cell thinking about how I had ended up there, thinking about how I had to change, how I never wanted to be in this position again, my first thought was that I wanted some.

I last had smack the day I was arrested, not before my arrest but after. I had been in the police station for hours being questioned repeatedly. I said nothing to them. I had been warned, you say anything and you are dead, simple as that. They repeatedly asked me about my family, their names, phone numbers, and addresses and I refused to say anything. Eventually, though, they tracked them down.

During the formal interview, when both my parents were present, they brought out the smack that I had in my pocket for personal use. When they brought it out, some spilled on the table. Now it was probably not noticed by anyone else but because I was starting the withdrawal process, the small bit of white powder that was on the table was the biggest thing in the room. I slowly moved my hands towards it, rubbed my fingers over it, and then rubbed it on my gums. Nobody noticed and this was the last time I had any.

It was now more than eight months later and I was still an addict even though I hadn't touched it. It just shows how strong addiction is. The prison system had another part to it for lesser offences committed by drug addicts and that was a six-month treatment programme that must be completed at a drug treatment centre.

But here I was, after all these months, still an addict. The guys quickly made a couple of cigarette joints and lit them. They licked the outside of the cigarette so that it would burn more slowly. After they had both had a few puffs each, it was offered to me. I took it straight away and inhaled deeply. I took a few puffs and passed it back. And that was it. I climbed back into my bed and drifted off. I awoke the next day wanting more, but there was no more to be had. It was gone. I was mentally craving it but had no physical withdrawals. I hadn't had enough to be physically addicted again.

A couple of days later, my bandages were taken off and I could see for the first time what they had done to my leg. It was a huge surprise that I saw only three small scars on my knee. Unbeknownst to me, I had received a new treatment. They had performed keyhole surgery on whatever was wrong with my knee. I now knew it was my knee that was the problem. I didn't know it before; I just thought it was my whole leg.

I was helped out of bed and, with some basic hand signals, was told to try to bend it. It was extremely painful. I was given a bit of paper written in Chinese but with some pictures showing me some basic exercises to do. It was never translated for me, but I could work out from the little Chinese that I had picked up over the last eight months, like the written numbers that informed me I had to do the exercises three times a day. So, I did the exercises and each day, I did them a bit more.

Every day, I would get out of bed and practice walking. Then I would start the bending exercises. One day, as I was allowed out of the cell to have a shower, I hobbled straight to the bath, filled it with hot water and slowly sunk into it. I felt like Cleopatra with her warm, ass milk bath! It was a huge luxury; I stayed in for as long as I could.

Chapter 21

I headed to the Old China Hand and met with Angus and Jim. After a couple of pints, Jim said:

'Party at Pokfulam this Saturday, fancy it?'

'Sure', I said.

'Cool. I'll pick you and Angus up in Central and then we'll all head there together'.

That Saturday, I met up with Angus and we headed up to Thingummy's for a pint before Jim picked us up. Angus had his gorgeous girlfriend, Daisy, with him. She had long, strawberry-blonde hair. She was tall -- at least six foot -- and had a smile you could just fall into. She was lovely. Whilst they went over to the park for a joint, I sat downstairs talking with Mr Lee. It was only 3.00 pm but he was already pissed. I say I was talking with him, I could never actually work out what he was saying.

Angus popped his head around the corner.

'Jim's here. Let's go.'

I staggered to my feet, as I had already sunk three pints, and went up the stairs holding my breath as always when I walked past the toilets.

Jim had gone to South Island School. His yellow jeep had a couple of other guys already in it, two rockers with long permed hair and a guitar bag slung over their shoulders. I introduced myself and I jumped into the back, Jim put his foot down and we headed west.

Pokfulam is an area with a load of high-rise buildings, an estate all to itself with a very large graveyard on one hill facing it and the sea right in front of it. It was a beautiful location. Everything was there that one needed including a shop selling alcohol.

Jim slammed on the brakes making us fall about laughing as we all clambered out to load ourselves up with enough alcohol to sink a platoon. I was last out of the store and Jim had already started to pull away. I had to run and jump into the back with Angus pulling me in.

It wasn't long until we had reached the party house. Somebody's parents were not going to be happy as the apartment was already trashed. I headed to the kitchen to find a cup, glass, bowl, whatever was available to pour my vodka and Coke into, when I met this amazing-looking girl leaning against the work surface.

She was stunning. I couldn't work out where she was from. It was as if she had the most amazing tan in the world. Her dark skin glowed. It had the silkiest texture and, with her mass of very dark brown curly hair falling across her shoulders, every time she laughed was completely transfixing. She caught me staring and smiled. Her white teeth nearly blinded me. It didn't take long for us to get to know each other.

'Hi, I'm Adelle.'

The next thing I know, we are in the toilets screwing.

She was an Australian of aboriginal descent. She went to South Island School so that was why I hadn't seen her before. We had an amazing night together but would I ever see her again? We just weren't in the same circles.

The party started to die down so some of us headed towards Wan Chai. Now Wan Chai wasn't somewhere I had done much socialising up to this point. It was the seedy part of Hong Kong, full of strip joints, tattoo shops, and triads. We all tried to keep away from the triads. They were notorious. But in general, if you didn't mess with them, they left you alone. The only time you would encounter them is if you caused any trouble at one of the local bars as they were all owned, operated and secured by the local gang.

There were always bunches of young triads hanging out on street corners. They stood out due to their clothing and their interesting habit of having a comb in their hair and a toothpick in their mouths. I had heard a lot of stories about them. But it just reminded me of the gangs in Glasgow; I don't know which were worse. We ended up dancing in the Pussycat Club until the early hours.

第22章

I had been in the hospital for about two months now and was dying to get back to prison. Some people around me were dying. It was never fun sitting in your cell with a dead body whilst they organised to have it removed.

I remember this one guy -- one of the first I saw in my hospital cell -- who died shortly after I arrived. It was at least a couple of hours before they finally came to take him away. He just lay there uncovered and dead until they ordered us to our beds whilst they picked him up and dumped him on a trolley and wheeled him out.

I don't know how many died or what they died of but there were a few. Some had died in the night and had probably been dead several hours before anyone took any notice of them. Some were old, but others were young. Some looked ill while others not so much. I suppose a lot of them had been inside for many years and this was to be their last cell. At least they died outside the prison if that was any consolation.

Eventually, I met with a physiotherapist who gave me a walking stick and taught me how to use it. After a few days of getting used to it, I was told that I would be leaving to go back to prison. At least I was leaving this place of death still alive.

Chapter 22

For the next few months, my life just turned into one long party. I would barely go home after my father found out I had been expelled. It was a good excuse for him to increase his drinking and so going home and sleeping on the couch with him constantly giving me verbal and emotional crap was just not a good option.

I did try and help, because his job had offered him more money to rent an apartment and because I was working at the estate agents, I was able to inform both my mum and dad before anyone else of any suitable apartments. Everyone I shared with him, he simply said no it wasn't what he wanted before he even looked at the information, let alone went along to any of the viewings I tried to set up for them. He was very good at making me feel like shit.

It was the beginning of March and the first party of the month was at my Dutch friend Florian's at Scenic Villas in Pokfulam. I ended up living in Pokfulam for a few weeks, either getting a lift to work or going by minibus. I either slept at friends' houses or sometimes I even slept under the buildings there where there was an amazing view of the shipping lanes in the South China Sea.

One day, my friend Kat and I sat in the middle of a friend's living room floor and drank alternative shots of tequila until we finished the bottle. That night, we spent under the buildings together, falling asleep on the pile of blankets we had taken down there. It was peaceful, I felt safe.

Towards the end of the month, Hong Kong got busier. There was a huge influx of foreigners on every corner, tram and ferry and in every pub and restaurant. The Hong Kong rugby 7s was approaching.

Lan Kwai Fong was as busy every night as it was on New Year's Eve. Out of the 5.5 million residents of the city, about 5 percent were expats but the week before the rugby 7s, it felt like that percentage had doubled.

Thingummy's was almost bursting at the seams. Lots of previous islanders who had now left school and gone to university had returned for the rugby, that was how big it was. Along with them came the teams from all over the world, their fans and the press. It was a week-long party until the two-day event even started.

The 7s were held at the Happy Valley football stadium and the tickets sold out months before. But I had been reliably informed that you could easily sneak in because the security wasn't that good. The first day I tried just that.

The year before, you may remember, the Berlin Wall came down and that had a direct effect on my entry to the Hong Kong 7s that year, or lack of it. The Soviet Union rugby team, or the Bears as they were known, were playing in the competition for the very first time so security, my friend told me, was stronger than in previous years and I was unable to sneak in.

With a group of other people who were ticketless, I spent the day travelling from pub to pub in Wan Chai: Neptune's, Big Apple and Joe Bananas. By the time I returned to Thingummy's, the rugby had finished for the day and I was hammered. There were so many parties that night, so I ended up back at someone's hotel in Admiralty, just outside Central, for a few more hours of drinking.

Bleary-eyed at 8.30 am, a group of us staggered from the shower to the hotel breakfast room where we happily dived into the buffet, waving off the staff who were trying to check our booking credentials. I knew the room number, ten of us did, but had no idea what name the room was booked under.

By the time the manager arrived in the dining room, I'd stuffed my pockets with croissants, butter and jam and had drunk enough coffee to get me through the day. It was then that someone, who had promised the night before, gave me a spare ticket that they had because their pal hadn't turned up.

So off we staggered towards the stadium once again. Jumping on a tram that took us to Sogo corner in Causeway Bay, I spotted the bomb man, a homeless guy who, for his own reasons, covered his whole body in electrical and engineering components.

We walked up the road to the stadium, the streets full of fans from all over the world. It was already warm but after walking into the stadium the temperature very quickly increased. This wasn't a rugby match; this was a festival.

A dozen national anthems were being sung from every direction. Flags from countries that I had no idea even played rugby were being waved. I'd been brought up mainly on the Five Nations and the occasional southern hemisphere game with the Lions. Those that were on the TV back in the 80s. I'd played for my school but had never attended a game as a supporter.

We had to walk the length of the stadium to get to the area where our contingent was based. All the school kids were behind the post at the far end. There were hundreds of them. The countless flags of so many nations pointed to the diversity of international students and the huge beer jugs from Carlsberg and San Miguel being carried by these students quite openly pointed to the complete apathy of those schools and our parents to underage drinking. I was

17 but a lot of the kids there were under 16, even under 15, and lots of teachers and parents were present.

So, we all got pissed together under the beating sun, buoyed by the electric atmosphere which at points seemed to have nothing to do with the sport on the field in front of us, but the sport of emptying the litre jugs of cold beer before they got warm.

Halfway through the day, I noticed a strange figure halfway up the stand walking up and down. No, he wasn't walking, he was marching in full soviet soldier uniform!

I had to investigate, I thought through my drunken, dehydrated haze. So, I climbed the stairs between the hysterical fans, stopping occasionally to speak to friends I hadn't met up with yet. All the time, out of the corner of my eye, I could see this figure was still marching up one way, doing a perfect about-turn, and marching the other way.

When I finally got to his level, I smiled as he marched towards me. All right, so he wasn't added security for the Soviet Union team. He was Nik who lived over the harbour in Tsim Sha Tsui and who went to another school. He and his family had visited Moscow months earlier and he had bought his authentic guard's uniform. His hat may have been a bit big but the whole outfit was as real as it gets.

We had a chat getting to know each other and I can't remember who came up with the crazy idea but before you could say Gorbachev, we were walking towards the team dressing rooms that were situated at the opposite end of the stadium behind the posts with some mashed together plan to pretend that he was Russian so that we could get to meet the Soviet team!

The changing rooms were a temporary building due to the number of teams that attended the 7s who couldn't possibly fit into the normal home and away rooms in the main stadium.

Living in Hong Kong as a teenager influences your ego. You're made to feel that you can do anything. I had gone from someone who used to hide in the woods or in the corner of the playground to being the autonomous CEO of everything that met me.

We could go anywhere and do anything; we were the elite. That inflated, or bloated, self-esteem was probably why we both thought we could do what we were about to try without a care in the world.

Maybe it was the air that we carried between us, but whatever it was, it carried the right amount of weight to get us through the line of security at the entrance of the changing rooms. When we spoke to one of them, he went away and was back within a minute with the team's captain. They could have named the team after this one guy. He was one of the biggest men I had ever seen in my life. He was probably the biggest bear I'd ever seen as well. As this man loomed towards us, someone who could crush the both of us in one of his gigantic hands, I had to become the person I was pretending to be. So, Nik and I stumbled through the next 30 seconds pretending to speak Russian.

It didn't go well. There are only so many 'Das' and 'Nyets' you can say before it becomes obvious. At that point, when it did, there was a smile that came across this giant's face and with a quick 'Dasvidaniya', he turned and left us half shaking and half laughing at ourselves.

第23章

When I got back to the prison, I went through the normal routine of a full search. I had got used to it a bit more by now but by no means was it a pleasant experience.

I was taken straight to the prison hospital and admitted because I still couldn't walk very well. But before I was fully admitted to the hospital ward, I had to wait to see the doctor. I quite liked seeing the doctor as he was the only person who spoke English. He didn't actually speak directly to me as he was a little odd; he would only speak in English so that I always knew what was going on.

When he eventually appeared, I was sent into his office. He was sitting there reading my notes. I couldn't make out everything he said but I picked up medial meniscus, ligament damage. It was the first time I had heard what was wrong although I didn't really understand what it meant. He then said:

'Won't be able to run again or walk uphill without assistance.'

That floored me. No one told me this; no discussion about what was to be done. As always, I wasn't allowed to talk so could not ask any questions.

I was then admitted back into the ward. Back into the ward with the huge weight of what he'd just said. It didn't sound right. It couldn't be correct. It didn't feel that bad but was it really?

No, I couldn't believe it, and I, at that very moment, was determined for it not to be the case. But all that had to wait as I had to deal with all the new faces in the ward. I had to size them up, see who thought they were in charge, see what the hierarchy was and see how I was going to fit into it.

The first thing I noticed was that the child rapist was not in the first bed anymore. A small, fat, strange guy with poking-out eyes was now the hospital boy. He brought me my white hospital uniform. All the beds were filled with new guys. I had to take the only free bed which was next to the wall at the far end. It was a proper hospital bed so was quite nice.

One of the new guys had his hand in the most amazing of devices. Connected at his wrist, a claw of steel was coming out with bits of wire attached to each finger. It looked like he had a new injury as his hand was in a bit of a state. Huge red scars covered his hand. I found out later that when he was being arrested, he put his hand through a window.

Another guy was a young triad. He was covered neck to feet with tattoos, the most amazing tattoos I had ever seen. Although they were not coloured, they were still amazing. His whole body was really one tattoo. A snake, a dragon and a phoenix wrapped their way around his body until their heads met at his stomach where there was a ball representing the sun.

But what was even more amazing was that he had the most chopper wounds to his body that I had ever seen someone alive with. They were everywhere, from his head across his chest, his right arm was nearly halved at the elbow, on his stomach, and on both his legs. He had been in a real fight and -- unbelievably -- had survived what must have been a horrific attack. He was only a small guy but must be one tough mother fucker. He was probably no risk due to his injuries.

The other two were nothing to talk about. In fact, I've forgotten about them.

We spent the days as we had the last time I was on the ward, rolling out toilet paper for the rest of the prison. I had developed a method where I could roll out a whole roll on my bed with each of the four squares slight offline with each other so that I could finish a whole roll and then just gently pull the paper apart. It sped up the process.

I had normally finished my quota before anybody else so I would usually take some of theirs to help them. Danny the tranny and one of his pals were brought to the ward daily. Danny had been released from his last sentence and was back in again on another petty theft charge, something like stealing makeup from a shop. He had been taking more of his hormone injections, so his breasts were quite impressive now.

I settled back into the hospital routine. I was now actually quite high up in the hierarchy in the hospital. I was known and, I suppose, a little respected. I did my push-ups and sit-ups even though it was still quite difficult because of my leg but it wasn't long before I was up to fifty push-ups again without much bother.

Different prisoners came and went. One I remember was a cannabis addict. In fact, he was one of the most addicted individuals I had ever met. He came in and it was obvious that he had been living rough for a very long time.

He was stripped and his body was caked in dirt. It was so thick that you thought that it was part of him. He was painfully thin and his hair was crawling. He was thrown into the shower room and had the hose turned on him. It was a sorry state to see.

After a few minutes, it was obvious that the dirt wasn't coming off, so he was given a hard bristled brush to scrub his body. He was so weak that he couldn't even do that, so the guards ordered the prison orderly to go in and scrub him. He was screaming out in pain but it had to be done.

Eventually, he was clean and then it was decided that his hair had to be shaved but because he was so wet a dry razor had to be used. He was left mostly bald with just a few patches of hair remaining. He was dried off and covered in powder. He wasn't allowed in the main cell so was put into one of the side cells where the damaged prisoners go. He was there a week before being moved out. He never made a sound. It was as if he wasn't there.

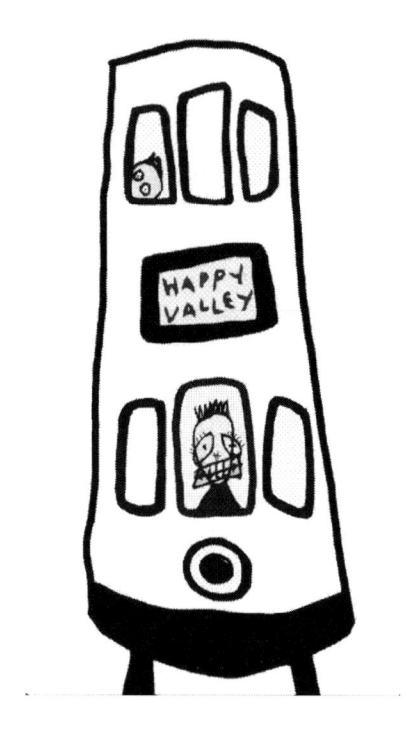

Chapter 23

For the next couple of months, it was a real struggle between work, exams and partying. Mornings were becoming more and more of a struggle, but there was no slowing me down. During the week, I was drinking at lunchtime on work days with one group of friends and then spending the evenings at Thingummy's with the crowd that hung out there.

The weekends moving closer to the summer were a mixture of houses, beaches and boat parties. Not to mention the girls as the following extracts from my diary will show:

'Thingummy's then boat party with Angus, Daisy, and some others.'

'Got sloshed and got off with Rachel from South Island School. Went to Thingummy's and laughed. Got very sloshed. Went home at 2330 and threw up at 2345.'

'Work, feel awful. What a hangover. Went to Thingummy's then went to Johns with Angus, Daisy, Zoe and Jim, drunk quite a bit. Then John, Angus and I went to Mad Dogs. Had something to eat, 2 pickled eggs. Then back to Thingummy's John changed some money there then we went to Wan Chai and got home at 0400.'

'Shopping in central with John and Angus. Me and John went to In Place then Thingummy's John with Kirsten and me with Lara. Then Mad Dogs. Three and a half pickled eggs then Wan Chai then home.'

'Went to Daisy's party, walking down the road Zoe and Jim drove past in Jim's Jeep I jumped into the back head first with feet hanging out back. Got to Daisy's. Daisy, Angus, Rochelle, Philip, John, Neris, Emma, Zoe and Jim had four bottles of champagne, a few bottles of wine and numerous Carlsberg and my big cigar. Had a lovely meal. Went up to Lara's party, got a lot drunker then went back to Daisy's. I brought Nik back with me and drank some more. Philip didn't like Nik so he took him to 7-Eleven and knocked the shit out of him. Nik comes back in tears. I took him back to Lara's then went back to Daisy's. Major argument breaks out. I get extremely pissed off and go to Lara's. Had great fun. Drank some more wine. Went to bed, living room floor at 5.30 am.'

'Met Phil 6.15. Beefy, me and Phil talking with Chinese people. Had a laugh. Went to In Place. Sloshed talking to Anna. I still like her, she still likes me. Had some snake wine with Phil left at 0430 went to Phil's, stayed the night, had a laugh.'

'Went to school and saw Mr Forse and Mr Harding handed in coursework to Mrs Caldwell, also had to finish coursework too. Me and John Thingummy's and then In Place. Phoned Allison and finished with her, her gran had just died, missed MTR and had to get the bus home. I still love Allison.'

'Work'.

'Awful hangover'.

'Got home from work and got a call from Allison she had to give me some work from school. I went up and met her. We had quite a good talk, close then she kissed me a lot then I went home. Phoned Melanie she's ill and Liz then a long talk with Adelle. Bed 9.30.'

'Me and John at Thingummy's 7.45, had one pint there then In Place, totally empty so we went to Bottoms Up [a topless bar] for a while to look at some tits then went back to In Place, went home at 12.'

'Lunch with Angus and sister, met John and Angus, then went to Scot's, Disco-Disco for a laugh then we went up to John's house and went swimming in his pool. Went back inside, freezing, talked a lot home at 0110. Angus knows Crossley in the navy.'

'Feel rotten!'

'Work/lunch at Old China hand skived some of the afternoon met Angus, Daisy, Emma, Phil and Rochell at the Go-Down then went to Marriott, John's room, got drunk then the In Place, Marlos' birthday, 16, talked to Kat, Adelle, Jo about Anna saw Anna gave her hug then left. Me, Angus, Phil and John then went to Bottoms Up and got hassled by Velvet again then went to Red Lips bar and left straight away. Went along to the Big Apple and stared at some tits. Angus nearly got into a fight. The Chilean barmaid gave Phil a naked lady earring, it made his day. Then we got the bus back to Wan Chai and went home sloshed, at 3.'

'Work first thing in the morning then went to see the Moscow State Circus in afternoon. It was brilliant. After, me, mum and my brother went for meal, got slightly tipsy, they went home and I went to Thingummy's saw Melanie Bev Zoe and Phil. Phoned Kat and went up to her house. We then caught a cab with her dog Sparky and went to Scenic Villas where Adelle was waiting for us. I then called Anna and asked if she wanted to come down, she did, so the four of us went under the blocks, we all had a laugh talking about everyone and everything. Kat and Adelle left at 10 so me and Anna stayed down we were talking a bit then we started talking about us had a very good talk she says she is very attracted to me but she is going out with Josh. It is very confusing but I think it won't be long until she dumps Josh and I can actually be with her at last. We finished talking at 12 so I left, she gave me a kiss goodnight on the lips. So I get taxi to Thingummy's, met Roger there it was very boring, so I left and got home at 1.30.'

'In very good mood today, woke up at 12 and went down to Scenic at 1.30, very fucking hot day had to take my trousers off to stay cool, met Roger down there, me and him went under blocks had a few fags and sunbathed a bit, found my navy knife under the blocks wow. Me and Roger then went up and called Ricardo he came down so we went under the blocks again Roger then came down with some lager so we drank that so I had to go up and buy some more, fucking sunny. Marlo and Anna then came down, looked great as always, I just wish I could be with her. Anyway we all had a laugh, Anna and Marlo left boohoo, but Jo then came down. Talked to her and Marlo about Anna. They both think that I and her will get together, wow. Jo left and Roger and Ricardo were talking about women, something about Ricardo and Roger's sister when she was only 13, had to leave at 6.30 to go to the airport, met Angus and Daisy, got a lift with Angus to Bonham Rd. Got a bus to Central, ferry to TST, bus to the airport, picked up dad, went home, watched Cocoon, sleep at 1145.'

第25章

The next prisoners to go into that side cell on the hospital ward were very different stories. Extremely sad. Because of newspaper censorship in prison, I never knew the true extent of their crimes.

Everyone who was sentenced to a life sentence spent their first night in one of these side cells under observation. Even though most will be expecting the sentence, it is always a huge blow when it happens.

Two boys around 15 years old were brought in. They had just been sentenced to life for murder. It was something that they had both been involved in, so they were sentenced together. That's all we could gather at the time. They were obviously very down and looked like two of the saddest people I had ever seen. They were put in the same cell with an extra mattress and fibreglass chair.

Lock-up was always at 7.00 pm. All the cells would be locked and we were allowed free time until the lights went out at 9.00 pm. After lock-up, all the prison keys were taken to the gatehouse and locked away, as I found out when I had to wait a couple of hours after having an asthma attack in my cell one night.

That night after lights out and we had all gone to bed, we heard that dreaded, familiar scraping noise. The orderly and I jumped out of our beds and ran to the cell door where there was a barred square gap in the solid metal enabling us to see across to the side cell which was fully barred with no solid metal.

What we saw will stay with me forever. The two boys were hanging there choking, clawing at their necks, eyes wide, spit coming out their mouths. The orderly hit the in-cell alarm and I shouted for the night guard. I shouted and shouted as they had a habit of just ignoring inmates. The orderly came and started shouting in Cantonese. The night guard then came running, but as he had no keys, he was off again. By this time the other prisoners were at the door trying to get a look, the orderly had seen enough and moved aside for someone else.

I just stood there frozen, watching them. I watched them die. Both had different twitches and spasms then one of them would find some more energy and start flailing again but then stop abruptly. The guard was back in a few minutes -- a few minutes too late -- with another guard but with no keys yet.

It was what seemed like another five minutes before the keys arrived. By this time, they had shouted at us to get back to our beds. It didn't really matter that the keys had arrived and, in all honesty, if the keys had arrived with the second guard, it probably would have been too late.

I tried to sneak another quick peek but there were too many guards, and I didn't want to get another shouting at, so I went back to bed. There was nothing to say, nothing to do, so we just went to sleep. I bet we all had strange dreams that night. I just thought of them both deciding to go out together. When had they decided? Was it during their trial? Had they made a pact that if they were found guilty, they would do it or was it a spur of the moment thing? Whatever it was, they were not there in the morning, nothing was ever shared with us and we knew we wouldn't be reading about it in the newspapers.

We talked about it amongst ourselves a few times but over the next few days, there was a quiet calmness in the hospital. We got on with our normal daily duties and that was that.

Chapter 25

After seven months of sleeping on the sofa at home and many friends' sofas dotted around Hong Kong, we moved to a new flat in Happy Valley. Just round the corner from the Hong Kong stadium where the 7s was held. The apartment block wasn't very high by Hong Kong standards, only twenty-five floors and we were on the fifteenth but, most importantly, I had my own room.

Of course, even though I worked as an estate agent and had shown my parents quite a few apartments, my dad turned them all down to choose his own. He should have stuck to engineering because the monthly rent was high for the size of the apartment.

Two days after we moved in, he went to work in South Africa for a few weeks. So, the apartment was temporarily a place of peace and for a while I felt at home.

Living in Happy Valley was a completely different experience from living in the affluent Mid-Levels area. Our apartment was clean and in far superior condition than Emerald Court. There was also natural light that came into every room as we weren't two floors underground but fifteen floors above it.

It felt more of a home especially as I had my own bedroom where I could lock myself away and listen to my music and I also I had somewhere to keep my clothes.

I'd really paid no attention to my clothes and had usually worn my friends' things because all my clothes had been stuffed in a suitcase under the sofa for eight months. I could now buy new clothes and toiletries.

It was a huge change for me, not just inside because the bustling centre of Causeway Bay was just a few minutes' walk and that gave a whole different energy and vitality to my life.

Getting to Central for work and Thingummy's was now just a tram ride away. 20 cents [2p] each way.

The next day, Roger and I headed down to Central and then hopped over to Ocean Terminal on the other side of the harbour as he wanted to go shopping. He bought a load of new clothes and got me a couple of new t-shirts and trousers as he quite rightly said I was starting to look a little rough and was embarrassed to hang out with me. The cheeky bastard was quite correct.

We headed to McDonald's for some sustenance and bumped into Melanie and Noya. It was totally unplanned but timed very well because Noya invited us to the bar where she worked as there was to be an exclusive secret concert that night. She gave us a couple of tickets and we all agreed to meet at Thingummy's at 6.00 pm before heading to the concert together.

Roger and I headed back to his to get ready. I was looking good in my new Giordano jeans and shirt; I even gave my trainers a wee clean! They had started to become a little offensive.

We headed down to Thingummy's to meet the girls. Roger had some cannabis with him and I did have a wee puff but it wasn't really my thing. Drinking was one thing my parents had taught me well.

When we met the girls, I sat in the bar talking to some other friends whilst those three disappeared to the wee park across the road for a joint or two.

They all returned rather stoned, Melanie a bit more than the others, after which we walked down to the MTR and headed over to Tsim Sha Tsui.

We got to the bar and there was a small queue outside so the others had another joint whilst we were waiting to get in. I said to Melanie to take it easy as she was already wobbling around quite a bit, but she said she was fine. She really didn't look it.

I was sticking to cigarettes which tonight had no danger of running out as there were a group of Salem Cigarette girls doing the rounds.

In Hong Kong cigarettes were already cheap but if you were in the right place at the right time and really didn't give a fuck what crap you smoked, you could smoke for free. There just so happened to be a bit of a marketing war between the Salem and Mild Seven cigarette companies so every night they would send scantily clad, gorgeous

Chinese lassies out on the town handing out free packets of cigarettes.

It wasn't just cigarettes, Haagen-Dazs also handed out free ice cream most mornings to commuters in Central, but I didn't like ice cream, couldn't smoke it!

Entering the bar, every table had 5 packets of Salem menthols along with accompanying matchboxes.

The bar was small and there were only around fifty people inside. I grabbed myself a beer. The others, being stoned, went and stood at the front of the stage which was a small semi-circle on the other side of the bar.

The four of us stood there for a while chatting, trying to guess who was coming on. There was a keyboard on a stand and a couple of guitars against the wall. Behind the stage, there was a door with a small window where I could see some people moving around.

Then one of the people came out of the door and we knew who we were about to be entertained by.

For the previous six or seven years, the music playing through the headphones attached to my portable cassette player consisted entirely of rock and heavy metal: Iron Maiden; Guns and Roses; Alice Cooper; and Deep Purple, amongst others.

It was 1990, I wore leather jackets, even when it was more than 20 degrees Celsius. So, what I was about to see, I thought, was completely out of my comfort zone. That zone was about to be invaded, literally.

Wearing a suit with huge shoulder pads and dark glasses, Vince Clarke came out and stood behind the keyboards. Immediately, the initial bars of A Little Respect exploded into the bar just as Andy Bell bounced onto the stage in a foot-long codpiece that nearly smacked me in the face.

Erasure proceeded to give us one of the best concert experiences ever. With constant costume changes which included ever-growing codpieces, they went through their most successful hits.

Unfortunately, Melanie didn't get to see the whole set as just into the third song she had a whitey. I had to escort her quickly outside where she showed a very little respect for the pavement by throwing up all over it. After taking her back inside after she had recovered and sitting her down in a corner where she promptly fell asleep, I rejoined the front of the crowd for the rest of the music.

There was an after party, but I decided to scoop Melanie up and take her home, via Thingummy's of course so that she could straighten up enough. I went in the taxi with her all the way up to her house on the Peak and then came back down to Thingummy's where I met up with the others who had a gift for me. The band had given everyone a free t-shirt and Noya made sure I got mine.

第26章

One day I was on the hospital ward and my number was called out.

'90760, choi sam' [Get dressed].

This shout by a guard was very unusual for me these days. In the beginning, it happened quite a lot and meant that I had a police visit. But I was now convicted so if it was a police visit, I was in deep shit.

Had they discovered a crime I had committed that I hadn't been sentenced for already? I didn't think so, well I hoped not, because some of them could carry a hefty sentence. So, I got dressed and stood next to the cell door like a good boy with my walking stick. The door was opened, and I was told to sit in the waiting room.

'Gwai Gi cho di'.

I waited and then was told to get up. I was handcuffed, which meant using my stick was very difficult, and I was taken outside. In the prison main gate area, there was a high-security prison van, the ones used for very serious offenders. I had never been in one before, so this was an interesting experience in one regard. The van had six doors that ran down the sides of a central corridor. Each door led to a tiny room that had a seat that was just big enough to sit down in but because I am tall, my legs were right up against the wall in front which was extremely uncomfortable for me with my bad leg.

I managed to squirm sideways in the seat to get somewhat comfortable. I wasn't comfortable at all though and that was when we weren't even moving. As soon as the van started driving, the movement sent waves of pain through my leg. We stopped for the obligatory check-in at the main prison gate hall. I was the only one in the van, so it was over quickly. The main gates opened, and we were off again ... a journey to who knows where in a tiny box stinking of what I did know.

It stank of piss, shit and body odour. The walls had been engraved with a thousand names and stories. Numbers were predominant I didn't know what they meant but some of them looked like the length of sentence; 10, 15, 30 were common figures. The box had a heavy weight of depression lingering as if thousands of souls were still trapped inside.

I could feel it all around me; I could almost taste it. It was thicker than the smell of human waste. It was the smell of human waste as if part of their souls had been discarded in this box as punishment and would live here forever to torment each individual for the crimes they had committed.

But with everything, the opposite must also be true. This was China and yin-yang is everywhere. So, for all those rightfully convicted of their crimes, some of the discarded pieces of souls were from those convicted of crimes they did not commit but were destined to spend 10, 15 and 30 years in prison for.

There was a tiny slot window but it had been graffitied so much that it was only letting in a tiny bit of light and making anything outside the window impossible to see.

That, I thought, was ironic. The countless souls who had marked graffiti on the inside, displaying their despair of being removed from the outside world, damaging the window so much that any last look at the world outside was stolen for them and for those who came after them. Was it done purposefully but subconsciously so that they could share some of their despair with others to lighten their own burden? I would never know but without the view, I had all this time to think about it.

I had to think of something. That was my safety net. Fill my head with thoughts of my own choosing so that my mind never for one moment had a time of emptiness that could be taken over with my own thoughts of despair. It was probably what had kept me from going completely insane so far.

When a person is blindfolded and sent on a journey to an unknown destination, some distance away and without any knowledge of what awaits them is unknown, it is hard not to slip into despair and panic. This box had witnessed all of that over the years. Maybe it had formed its own soul net to capture the damaged souls. Maybe it fed off them.

The van stopped. The door to the box opened. It was then that I had realised that throughout the whole journey, I had forgotten the pain in my leg. I thanked the box as I painfully straightened my leg, and the pain came back. I thanked it for helping me to forget. I hobbled up and caught myself from falling with my walking stick and shuffled down the corridor to the back of the van, immediately wincing at the bright day outside.

When my pupils had finally dilated enough, I was able to admire my surroundings. A car park with mowed lawns, trees and shrubbery. Behind it, a single-storey, red-brick, quaint, old building. I was taken to the building, through the reception area and then into a large room. I finally realised where I was and what was happening. The room was full of equipment that was being used by lots of people, most of them were old and accompanied by someone in a uniform. It was a physiotherapy centre.

I was amazed again at the level of care I was receiving. Nobody looked at me this time as I was taken shuffling to the end of the room and introduced to a Chinese woman in a uniform who was going to be my physiotherapist. Nobody was interested in me. They were all too engrossed in what they were doing to even notice me and the two prison guards coming in.

My physiotherapist, Miss Chan, was next to a set of stairs that went up and down to nowhere, quite reminiscent of my thoughts during the journey here. She explained to me that she had been tasked to get me to be able to walk up and down stairs unaided. So that's exactly what we did for the next hour. Up and down the stairs.

The only stairs that I had attempted recently were the steps into the van and back out again. I hadn't realised how bad my knee was. The doctors had said that I wouldn't be able to walk uphill unaided or o ever run again. At that time, I told myself that they were wrong and I would achieve it all. Now I was realising how difficult it was going to be. Because I had not used my leg for over two months, the muscles had wasted. My knee hadn't been bent in all that time either.

On the first attempt, Miss Chan took my stick away from me and I started to panic. I almost fell but managed to grab the handrail that accompanied the steps all the way up and down again. There I stood, with both hands grabbing the same rail, both legs wobbling and then shaking.

It was a humbling experience and, for once, I almost felt my resolve crumbling. My eyes welled up with tears which I managed to get rid of quickly. It was my first real emotion for the first time in months; I wasn't going to allow that to happen.

Over the next hour, we worked on me trying to lift my leg up to the first step. When that had been achieved, I had to try and put my weight on it. I tried and I failed. At the end of the hour, I was feeling pathetic, lost and a complete failure. But Miss Chan told me that this was just the beginning and that I would be coming every week until I had succeeded and that it was her job to make it happen. I stumbled back to the van at the end of the session with a mixture of emotions.

First, I was going to get out of prison once a week for the foreseeable future, which was a positive even though I would have to go through the whole search procedure when I got back. It wasn't as bad anymore; I had somewhat got used to it having been through it so many times now. It wasn't pleasant and it wasn't my first choice of how to finish a fun day out, but it was worth it.

I was going to get weekly what some of the guys inside would only get after ten or fifteen years. The only view that they would have of the outside was the top of a solitary tree that could only be seen at one corner of the wall and only if you were in that part of the prison.

I realised that I was going to the physiotherapist only because the prison needed me to be able to walk up and down stairs so that I could go back to the general population. On the one hand, they were helping me to get better but, on the other, they were helping me to go back into hell. I was a someone in the prison hospital and a no one in general population. I also wanted to get better too.

But I was stuck with the previous realisation that when I got better enough to go back, I may be sent back to the hospital in an even worse condition if I even made it back to the hospital and not out of the prison feet first. This was a very real possibility in my mind.

Chapter 26

The anniversary on 4 June 1990 was a big day for everyone in our part of the world, as well as elsewhere. All schools were closed so that students could attend and everyone I knew attended. It was because of the students and what they had tried to peacefully achieve that we were all here together.

We marched and sang from Admiralty all the way to Victoria Park. Some said 50,000, some said 150,000, all I knew was that the whole route was full of people and that the roads were wide enough for 200,000 people to have been there that day.

The crowd displayed a multitude of emotions that all became as one when we reached Victoria Park in the early evening and a carpet of flames from candles filled our vision. It was peaceful and serene but then a friend said that it was all kicking off at the Chinese Embassy near the racecourse at Happy Valley so a few of us headed over there to see what might be taking place.

A few people sat next to the embassy behind a sheet demonstrating their personal thoughts and sang slogans whilst the police stood there wondering what to do.

We decided to head to Thingummy's. It may have been the most sombre we have ever been in Thingummy's, generally silent, washing our own thoughts away with the cheap beer.

The next day, I headed over to Tsim Sha Tsui for a friend's birthday and had shark's fin soup for the first time, I have to say it did actually taste delicious. Afterwards, Melanie and I headed to the Body Shop so she could buy girls' stuff.

She made me sniff all the different soaps and, after about ten minutes, I was as high as a kite, almost tripping with the intoxicating fumes. She always smelt sensational, now I knew why. But she was like my best friend, a sister, nothing more. We were best friends, always had been.

The day after that, Melanie and I were back in Central with some other friends. The conversation was all about sex, it must have been the summer heat doing its magic on us kids!

At 7.00 pm, we all headed to a fairly new bar in Lang Kwai Fong called the Beach Hut. Before being allowed entry, we had to get membership cards, no idea why but they wouldn't let you in without one. When we eventually got our IDs, us underage kids with our now fake IDs created by a bar, we went inside and were given free Long Island Iced Teas. It was my first and I enjoyed it, so Melanie and I got a few more.

The most gorgeous lassie I knew called Jo was there. She was beautiful, I had admired her for a while so, bolstered by my new cocktail, I moved over to say hello and offer her a drink. Then we kissed. We kissed and danced all night long. I couldn't have been happier; life was getting better and better.

The next day, I was fired.

Of course, I knew I would be eventually. I turned up most days still drunk from the night before and sometimes would head straight to the toilet to sleep. I was caught in there three times recently so I knew my time would be up, sooner or later.

So, to celebrate, we went to Thingummy's and got very drunk, for a change.

第27章

In the hospital one day, I heard that the guy who had so maliciously attacked me on the football pitch had just returned from his appeal hearing. He had been serving an eight-year sentence for armed robbery. I found out that the appeal hadn't been brought by him and his solicitor but by the prosecution who had wanted a longer sentence, and they had won. He came back with a 15-year sentence instead and had been moved into the 'prison inside the prison', the secure category A unit for the seriously bad guys.

This was somewhat of a moment for me to cheer about. At first, I cheered because I had this crazy idea that his sentence had been lengthened because of what he did to me, but also that I wouldn't be anywhere near him again as he was in the nuthouse.

The category A block was a creepy looking place. It had an air of the super evil about it. We were in a maximum-security prison with huge walls, fences and gun towers. Even the visiting rooms were high security with a bomb-proof glass between you and your loved ones and where you could only use a phone to communicate with each other.

The category A unit was behind another set of fences in a corner of the main prison. It had its own gun towers. The only exercise places for the inmates were separate cages, although there was one big cage where they could occasionally play a sports game together if it was believed that they weren't going to try to eat each other!

I had heard that they still had the execution chamber in there and that you could see it; it was still in working order just in case it had to be used. They used to hang people in there and still had the ability to reinstate the death penalty if need be.

Allegedly, you could see the whole set-up, minus the rope, it was next to the TV room and the prisoners were made to walk past it every day, as if to show them how lucky they were that they weren't being put to death by hanging.

The problem for a lot of the inmates in that block was that, in 1997, only a few years away, Hong Kong was going to be handed back to China. In fact, it was on a lot of our minds. Even if I had spent my whole six-year sentence there, I should be released before the handover. However, there was always a real chance that something could happen in here that would cause my sentence to be increased, keeping me here until the Red Army marched across the New Territories and took control once again.

China had made various promises as to how things would be done after the handover but not many were fully buying it. Many of the Hong Kong Chinese were trying to get out. The word on the street was that the UK government were selling UK passports for £1 million.

The joint declaration had been signed by the UK and China in 1984 for the hand-over in 1997 but it wasn't until the terrible events of June 1989 that most people woke up to the reality of it all.

Forty years beforehand, Chinese people trying to escape Mao Tse Tung's socialist revolutions extermination squads fled over Hong Kong's borders and many of them had been hiding there ever since. Some of them believed that the Chinese government still had a desire to hunt them down and punish them, so they were petrified with what happened on 4 June 1989, as were the rest of us.

I had taken part in protests not knowing how close I may come to being imprisoned by that regime. Afterwards, there was a huge panic amongst Hong Kong citizens and what became known as the 'brain drain' took effect. What it meant was that anyone with the money and contacts to get out of Hong Kong with their family to a relatively safe country elsewhere did so.

For that reason, there became, literally overnight, a huge opportunity for anyone looking for a job. Companies were so desperate to hire people that they would give you a minimum of a two-month contract that meant that you would get paid for at least two months before they sacked you.

On Saturday mornings, the main local English newspaper, the South China Morning Post contained a 'Classified Post' which contained the job section. It was huge. Dozens of pages advertising jobs from the president of huge multinational companies down to messenger boys. For even the lowest level employees, the salaries were attractive.

One of my previous classmates from school was looking for a secretarial job. She attended more than seven interviews and was offered the jobs but turned them all down until she got a job which had an office with a harbour view! She was only 17 years old but secured a high salary as well as a view.

One company that we all worked at was called something like Worldwide Finance and had its office in Central district. It was a sales job, selling things like stocks, shares and futures and none of us had any idea what we were doing.

After a few of my friends had worked there, I went for my interview and got the job on the spot. It had a great wage and no fixed hours to work. Basically, they were hoping that we would go out to our rich parents and get them to invest in the company's portfolio. But none of us ever did. It was open 24 hours a day as they were engaged in stock markets around the world. I sometimes went in after being in the pub to take heroin in the toilets and watch the rolling news come in on the printers. There was a room full of printers that would churn out news from different agencies from around the world: Associated Press, some French stuff, CNN, the BBC. I worked there for the allocated two months, got paid, and left.

Chapter 27

My dad's brother Malcolm arrived for a visit, so I had to spend the day with my family meaning I had to miss Melanie's birthday meal.

I hurried from the flat in Happy Valley down to the MTR. When I got into the In Place, Melanie was the very first person I bumped into. She was standing at the bottom of the stairs and I could immediately tell that she was pissed off with me.

'I am so sorry,' I said.

'You missed my birthday! How could you', she replied.

And then she stormed off. I was gutted, I felt so bad. She was my best friend in the world. She meant everything to me and I had put a wedge between us. I wandered off to the bar and got my pint glass. It was there I bumped into Ricardo.

'What's up, mate', he said as Ricky the Barman poured me a pint. I told him what had happened and he said, 'I know, mate. She told me'.

I was so upset I was nearly in tears.

Then he said:

'Listen, I've got something that will make it better. Come on.'

So, I followed him through the fire escape and up to the alley at the back. We burst through the fire door and were in the back alley. As we walked down the alley, we passed a few couples engaged in teenage activities -- kissing, fondling, blow jobs, etc. -- until we reached a quiet spot. He pulled out his wallet, opened it and produced a small folded up piece of paper in a rectangle, it was very neat.

He said, 'Try some of this; it will make everything feel better. Get a banknote and roll it up.'

As I went into my pocket and fished out some cash, he opened the packet and showed it to me.

'What is it', I asked.

'Heroin,' he said, 'Number 4. Snort some up your nose.'

I had no idea what heroin was, but I did what he said. I put my rolled up $10 note to my nose lowered my face down to the packet until the note was just about touching the powder and snorted.

The white powder jumped off the packet and raced up the money tube deep into my nose. It hit the back of my throat and I gagged. It was instant. I managed to control my gag and then felt the rush. Wow. I tried not to be sick and then this huge rush of euphoria washed all over me. It filled every part of my body in an instant.

I kept gagging as some more dripped down my throat. My eyes were watering but I felt fucking brilliant. It was getting stronger and stronger. I felt completely wasted, happy, high. All stress and sorrow had left me. I felt amazing. Don't know how I got back into the In Place -- my face was zinging, waves of tingling all over my body.

I found myself in front of Melanie. She asked me if I was okay because my eyes were bloodshot from the gagging. I told her I felt amazing and that I had just taken heroin. She went ballistic, screaming at me about how stupid I was. I stopped hearing her and I went dancing. And that's the last I can remember.

第28章

After a few days back in the prison hospital, it became apparent that the new guys' noses were a little out of joint because I was taking control of the place. They started to be a bit aggro with me over the smallest of things.

But, as in everyday life, the little things started to build until one day the small chopped up triad squared up to me and said, 'Fighting' to me.

First, I just looked at him and thought, 'Why?'

Then I looked at him again, with all his fresh scars and his arm with metal rods sticking out of it and turned and told him to fuck off.

He said, 'Fighting' again to me. His pal with the smashed-up hand was also trying to stir things up. I looked at him and said that I didn't want to hurt him, but he wouldn't listen, so I said, 'Okay, fighting'.

So, we went toe to toe and it must have looked comical. Me, standing at just over six-feet, and this wee waif of a triad held together with stitches and steel rods dancing around each other.

I was trying to find somewhere to hit him that wouldn't damage him too much. He was wildly swinging at me with his one nearly good arm but kept on missing. I decided that his head wasn't badly damaged, so I punched him in the face. He flew back against the wall and slumped to the floor.

I said 'Enough' but the daft wee guy got back to his feet and shouted, 'Fighting' again. I sighed and punched him in the face again, this time not too hard; just enough to knock him back and hopefully get him to stop. But I was beginning to see the ox heart that he had inside that crisscrossed, scarred body.

That was probably why he had survived his previous attack. I just started punching him in the face. His body being far too damaged for me to sink my fist into. I stood there punching him for about thirty seconds before I decided that he'd had enough. Sure enough, he backed off.

It was a strange feeling afterwards. I had obviously marked my presence as the top guy in the hospital ward and he probably felt low that he lost. But I quickly wanted him to feel that I held no ill feelings towards him. About ten minutes after the fight, having given him time to lick his wounds and recover, I asked him if he was okay.

Over the next few days, our friendship repaired as he finally realised that I was a bigger personality than him and there was nothing that he could do.

After a few more visits to the physiotherapist, my leg was a lot better. I was able to get up and downstairs with minimal difficulty. So, it was decided that I was to go back into the general population. This was not a move that I was looking forward to. I was now more vulnerable. People had come and gone so the whole social structure would have changed.

Chapter 28

My Dad finally left to go to South Korea to work for a few months. He'd been home for too long this time and it was really taking its toll on all of us.

When I was younger, he would be away for ten months of the year and home for perhaps three or four weeks. It was really challenging but it was manageable. Although I did miss him and, from a small age, really needed him, he never once kicked a ball with me and I can only remember going fishing with him once. The rest of the time was taken up with doing repairs around the house, drinking and going to the shops.

Then he was home for most of the time as he had a 9 to 5 job, only going away if there was a major issue he needed to attend to at a dry dock somewhere around the world.
That didn't change our interactions though. He had no time for me even though he had more time for me. We had done a few family things together, only a few. He had taken me to the pub once when I had first got to Hong Kong. I was 16 and that was the only way he could think of to engage with me. Is it any wonder why I sought out companionship at Thingummy's?

After he left for South Korea, I took my Uncle Malcolm to the Temple Street market. He had been with us for a few days now and, being somewhat of a polyglot, he now spoke more Cantonese than the limited amount I had learned in over half a year.

We sat at a café and had fresh shrimp, from still swimming around in a huge tank to swiftly being scooped up in a large metal net straight into a massive wok atop a furnace to onto your plate in around a minute. Heavenly.

As we walked down through the rows of t-shirts and copy watches we planned the next stage of his visit. A trip to China.

It was only recently that China had opened its doors to foreigners so it would be quite the journey. We decided that we would get the train to Guangzhou which only took four hours. We agreed to go early the next day. I'd never been before so I was excited.

I took Malcolm back to Central and I headed up to Thingummy's where I met up with Melanie. We had a chat about me taking the heroin, I promised not to do it again. I really didn't know what it was and I was sorry that I had missed her birthday lunch. We hugged and I headed home early to get ready for tomorrow's early start.

We got up at 6.30 am and headed to the station. So, it wasn't going to be as easy as we thought. We missed the first train and had to hang around until noon for the next one. You had to go through customs before getting on board as the train wouldn't stop at the border but would continue into China and would only stop again once safely across where we were asked to show our papers whilst still on the train.

Even though the train didn't stop at the border, it was obvious when we crossed. The buildings changed from all modern and looked after to older ones with broken windows. It was these small details that I noticed whilst staring out of the train window.

After a slight immigration problem due to my Hong Kong ID card being only a temporary one which should have been replaced, Malcolm and I walked out into the absolute wonder of Guangzhou.

The station was massive. As we had been delayed due to my ID card issues, all the other passengers had already left so Malcolm and I walked through the station practically alone. There was a huge line of ticket desks with only a handful of passengers. It was a very strange apocalyptic scene. Coming from Hong Kong which was constantly filled with humanity, the station was eerily quiet.

Then we walked through the doors into that lost humanity. I simply had never seen so many people before. In front of the station was a multiple football pitch sized area that held the population of an average-sized city. Everybody looked as though they were camping as they were all sitting on mats and rugs, families with bags surrounding them and their cooking stoves. It was surreal, a village pub moment when the music goes off and everyone turns round to look at you.

We were suddenly the most exciting thing to be seen in Guangzhou. I was wearing a t-shirt and shorts and, within seconds, I had two wee old ladies smiling next to me and staring at my legs. First, one of them touched my arm and, whilst we were smiling at each other, her wee pal had reached down to stroke my legs.

It was the hair that they were excited about. They were like two wee schoolgirls who had found a big hairy dog they wanted to pet. After gently untangling their fingers from my strange foreign coverings they then started saying:

'Changey money, changey money?'

I had done some exchange rate calculations before we arrived. After asking them how much for Hong Kong dollars, their happy faces turned sad as they were looking for British pounds or US dollars.

Saying goodbye, we headed across the field of families who all seemed to be waiting to go nowhere. We reached the other side of the field to where the city began.

Before we could head off towards the hotel that we had booked, first our eyes were drawn to a wee crowd at a street corner. Looking around, nearly every corner had the same kind of small crowd of people huddled around a pretty rough looking person who was sitting on the ground with a large blanket folded over.

On seeing us, one guy reached towards the cover and, giving a wee look around, pulled it back to reveal which could only be described as a zoological horror show.

Trying not to recoil in absolute disgust, I only quickly scanned the selection of massive bear claws that looked stomach churningly fresh along with various other body parts recently procured from the Chinese countryside. He quickly realised that these souvenirs weren't really what we were looking for, so he repacked his endangered butcher's shop.

We headed off towards our hotel with the wee leaflet that we had been given by the booking agent in Hong Kong. Everything here was in massive proportions. Modern but also old at the same time.

There were trolley buses that looked like they were older than the Hong Kong trams, no cars but old trucks and bikes. Bikes as many as the road was wide. Thousands everywhere and every one of their riders turning their heads to look towards us. School kids, businessmen, even some with baskets on the back with their pet dogs being taken for a cycle. All the dogs looked the same, I suppose that's Communism for you.

The Linhua Hotel was advertised as a 3-star hotel but it was so grand I expected to see corgis running down the marble hanger that was the main entry hallway.

We had to be taken to our room. I said we could find it but the lady at reception insisted. So dressed for Glastonbury rather than Buckingham we followed the lady down the hallway, and another, then a lift, across a huge central circular auditorium, down another corridor and then what felt like thirty minutes later arrived at our room in what seemed to be an empty hotel.

After a rather fast round of bathroom needs, we were off back out the door quick enough to remember the sequence of our entry. It was early evening, so we went off in search of somewhere to eat.

For the first time in my life, I was in a city where nothing made sense to me. Every sign meant nothing. There was no script anywhere. Even in Hong Kong, most signs had their English equivalent underneath but here it was all Chinese characters that made absolutely no sound in your mind when you looked at them.

The walk was worth it as we discovered some incredibly beautiful sights including the White Swan Lake and hotel. But we were so hungry that we had to finally resort to the next place we found which turned out to be a five-star restaurant serving a multi-course meal. After five courses with accompanying beer, we were full and asked for the bill. We could eat the whole meal again and still it wouldn't have cost anything near to what it was worth. It was so cheap. We headed back to the hotel and finally crawled into our beds and fell asleep.

The next day, we visited the Whampoa Pagoda. We managed to climb up the crumbling wooden stairs to the top on the ninth level which had a fantastic view of

Guangzhou. It showed every year of its 390 years and it didn't look like it would survive many more if it didn't undergo some major renovations.

We went for a wee bite at lunch. I wanted to hire a bike to tour the city and my uncle wanted to go and have a wee look around the shops. So, we agreed to meet back at the White Swan hotel and lake at 4.00 pm.

I had seen where to hire a bike, so I went and got one for a few hours even though I only wanted it for an hour and half or so. I must be honest and say I was feeling a bit wobbly at first as I tried to move from the edge of the road and into the flow of thousands that were zipping past me like a river in full flow. But once I had stopped wobbling, it was super exhilarating.

I was chatting with so many people, in the way that people unfamiliar with each other's language do. Old men, workers in overalls, businessmen and lots and lots of schoolchildren all tried to sidle up to me for a chat. I had to keep my ears open for the ting ting of the trolley buses and keep clear of them as they went wherever they wanted to with little care for the cyclists surrounding them.

At 4.00 pm I got back to the café, but there was no sign of Malcolm. After two hours of waiting, he finally arrived. He had been walking down the street when two people had approached him to ask if he wanted to teach English to some local kids. So, being him, he said yes and had been at an English school all afternoon and had plans to go back again the next day.

We left early that morning and headed towards the marketplace. Passing lots of people taking their pets for a cycle I would soon realise that perhaps all wasn't as happy in puppy-land as I had believed.

On entering the market, we were wrapped up in the scent of what made this part of the world so famous, with barrels open at the top filled with all the most exotic spices you could ever imagine. Then there was the fruit and vegetables. Apples the size of watermelons and limes the size of apples and green knobbly things straight out of Star Trek. All of this wasn't something that was interesting to me, I enjoyed it but I wasn't a cook.

It went on and on and on until we got to the seafood and meat section. That's when things changed, now I was interested.

They weren't pet dogs.

It was like a miniature zoo where the animals weren't two by two but packed by the dozen into cages, tanks, and buckets. It was a horror show. Most of the meat was, um, fresh. A lot of it wasn't. there were bits and pieces of every kind. At one table, I found what I thought were the stripped hind legs of deer, but I was wrong, they were penises.

We didn't buy anything for dinner but headed back to check out of the hotel and catch the next train back to Hong Kong.

第29章

I was moved back into the general population.

Then….

'Fight!'

The first time I went for a shower, three guys came in with socks filled with soap and attacked me. The attack seemed to just be a warning as it lasted for only a few seconds before they all ran out again.

'Fight!'

Walking back to my cell one night, I just felt something was brewing. One of the big brother's lieutenants, out of character, started walking towards me, I looked down and saw the sharpened toothbrush. As soon as I saw it, I kicked out at him, catching him in the mid-thigh. He yelped, fell to the side and the alarm went off.

He dropped the homemade knife; it was kicked towards another cell just before the guards came running round the corner. I ducked into my cell. No one said anything; no one saw anything.

That night I started sharpening my own toothbrush against my cell wall.

I never finished it, never got to use it. I suppose I was lucky. I never wanted to hurt anyone, let alone kill them, I think?

The last fight had been brewing for a while. By now they had realised that maybe I wasn't as weak and pathetic as perhaps I appeared. It was back to the psychological torture that had caused me so much anguish that very first night over a year ago.

Back then, it was mostly just noise with a few words I partially understood. Now it was mostly words that I was familiar with but didn't understand what they actually meant, interspersed with the usual 'fuck you gwai gi'. The cold and hunger blocked most of it out, so I slept through most of it.

The mornings may have been freezing cold, but hunger and need made me get out of bed. I was now into such a routine that I'd wake up five minutes before the radio came on and would have toileted, washed and brushed my teeth before that nauseating and still unintelligible ranting came on each day.

I had to prepare my cell every morning now to protect my belongings from the various bodily liquid attacks that I either suffered whilst there or would find when I returned in the evening. I had also learned to hide my most treasured items as many had been stolen previously using string and hooks that others could use if they got the chance.

Once my three rough blankets had been folded and placed on top of my matt and on my hard bed I started exercising, trying to get all my stiff cold joints working so that I was physically ready for any attack.

I would get my sharpened toothbrush, now with a cloth attached at the handle end for extra grip and slip it into the hem of my shirt where I had loosened the stitching just a tiny bit. I had practiced taking it out time and time again in my cell so felt I would be able to get to it quickly in a fight situation. Just as I was about to do it, the guard came round the corner, so I dropped to the floor instantly and started doing push-ups, still with it in my hand.

The guard shouted something. This wasn't the normal routine. I heard his keys, then I looked up and other guards came round the corner, it was a cell search. They were quick, I wasn't. Taken completely off guard, I told to get out of my cell still with the knife in my hand.

I did what I was told, pretending to concentrate on buttoning my shirt with the knife hidden. I crossed and turned with my back to the windows across from my cell. With the most concentrated movement of my entire life, I flicked my knife towards one of the open windows. By 'open', I mean it was open by as much as 3 inches. I couldn't even look, I could only listen, I heard nothing.

The knife was either lying somewhere in full view or had miraculously flown through the window. I had no idea.

Cell searches were random, but only happened when the cells occupants were present and were never done thoughtfully. The cells were completely stripped by the guards. They threw everything outside the cell so that they could then search every inch of the inside.

You were then made to strip all your clothes off, everything, and then go back inside your cell whilst the guards searched every part of your belongings. They ripped books apart, squeezed your toothpaste out, broke open your soap and if you were lucky enough to have any biscuits or crisps left from your monthly wages, they opened them and spilt the contents onto the floor.

Once they'd finished, they would get you to pick up everything and take them back into the cell. Everything had to be put back in order and any mess they had made cleaned up. It's done for a couple of reasons, first to find contraband and weapons but also to demoralise you. It doesn't always do the first, but it always does the second.

That morning, it delayed breakfast, so no one was happy.

When we were all back in our cells and the doors were locked again, the unhappy mutterings started. Someone always had to be blamed when things went wrong. It was as if people needed to direct their anger at someone. That someone always tended to be me. Shit flows down, as they say.

The first 'Gat gwai' came out followed by another and another. These were interspersed by the more fashionable 'Giordano', the fashion brand with a frog for a logo. 'Gat gwai' meaning frog, or big mouth, and, in Chinese prison culture, grass.

I was never a grass, even right at the start when I was withdrawing and put under immense pressure by the police, I'd never opened my mouth. I'd seen what happened to a grass in here. It always seemed to be incredibly well planned. This was when you would really see the power the big brother had in here.

From day one, my eyes had been everywhere taking in every detail of day-to-day life. Any unusual movement always caught my eye immediately.

Big brother's cellmate, righthand man and bitch was Maa Lau [monkey boy]. Small with big ears, he looked as he acted. Anything he did was at the behest of his master, he never acted on his own.

It didn't take me long to work things out. Over the last year, I had witnessed dozens of sudden explosive acts of absolute violence. Unless you've been in a maximum-security prison with the most violent of offenders, your only experience of fights will be the two or more people shouting at each other and then rolling around on the ground together, mostly under the influence of alcohol.

Maximum-security prison violence is immediate and furious and never clumsy and uncontrolled. It goes from zero to 100 instantly and the target is usually severely injured, hospitalised or quite simply left dead. But you never know the outcome, if you're not involved you know exactly what you must do and you do it instantly.

When the alarm goes off, every prisoner must put their heads down with their hands over their heads, onto a table if you are sitting or flat on the ground if you are outside. You're not allowed to look or talk or move until told to do so. You were not allowed to look especially when the guards start their feverish beatings of all the prisoners involved. I'd even seen, because of course you did try and look, one guy with blood pouring out of him getting beaten by the guards until they realised that he wasn't moving anymore.

If it was a serious fight and someone had been badly injured, then any other prisoners not involved were removed from the area and it wasn't until a couple of weeks later when the fighters returned to general population that you could see if any of them were missing. But you never truly knew what happened to the severely injured. Either they were in hospital, transferred to another prison or dead.

But one thing was for sure, any attacks always had to be approved by the big brother. Many of the fights weren't for retribution or arguments from just the usual day to day goings on within the prison population, they were from information provided by different guards. Maa Lau was the only prisoner that would ever get up out of his seat during Saturday or Sunday to go and speak to one of the guards when we were together in the main dining hall to play games, read and share biscuits and crisps from our wages. Once I'd seen a guard gesture for him to come over.

I obviously never knew what was said, but most of the time, a day or so later, someone would be attacked by one or more of the big brother's soldiers. Random fights were always quickly resolved by the guards within seconds. Fights sanctioned by the big brother tended to happen just as the guards, for some unknown reason, left the area for a few moments. They would never leave their posts normally, only just before someone was attacked, and then they would take their time to do anything about it.

After the cell search that morning, I knew that there was something brewing.

Marching to the dining hall for breakfast I could feel a hundred eyes burning into my back. I could feel and hear their whispered threats. Every day in prison was dangerous, not knowing what was going to happen. Today I knew something was going to happen and somehow, bizarrely, that felt safer.

It happened in the dining hall. I was last in line and my food was taking longer than usual to come from underneath the hatch. There was never a fight before food, it was always after so that no one went to solitary on an empty stomach.

I glanced round and was confronted by a wall of bowed heads but with eyes facing towards me as mouthfuls of rice were being shovelled rapidly. I panned right to the big brother's table. Our eyes locked together.

Bang.

'On Chaan'.

I jumped higher than my internal tough guy wanted to and turned to pick up my plate of bread and cheese and my cold mug of putrid milk tea. I headed towards my table planning to quickly devour my appetiser for the day ahead.

Two guards to my right looked back to me but over my shoulders, he must have got out of his seat as soon as I reached mine. In one of those freezeframe moments that might happen in the cinema, I looked down at my unopened cheese and sighed as I realised I wasn't going to get a chance to eat it, looked back at the guards and heard him behind me, leapt to my feet and swung round ready for him, all in the same second.

It was Maa Lau, the big brother's bitch, and he fought like one too. He did land a punch in my face but that was it. I was an idiot though as while I was focusing on him, I forgot to check who else was there and, within that first second, there were others.

Then it went wild, for a few seconds before the alarm sounded and the guards were on top of us. I don't know if I was disappointed, maybe a little bewildered even, but I had expected more. As I was being dragged off to one side by three guards and being kicked punched, elbowed and generally battered, I was almost glad for each hit as it proved that I was still there.

So many times, I'd had nightmares of being killed, brutally stabbed to death, left lying in pools of blood. crying out for my mummy. Many of those nightmares had happened multiple times a week. Each one had a slight deviation from the last as if I was some kind of sick movie director trying to make the next scene just that little bit more horrific and graphic, so deliciously presented for the hungry horror viewers.

Why didn't they just kill me? They had killed others. The alarm bell went off a minimum of three or four times a day. I'd seen ambulances and even coffin vans pull into the prison courtyard. I'd seen multiple stabbings, once between two guys who shared a cell together and the amount of blood could only really mean someone had been thoroughly drained. Hangings, wrist cutting and my all-time favourite, how the fuck could you do that to yourself, neck cutting were as regular as a Chinese festival.

Standing in the governor's office I knew that I was at the end. They were going to kill me. I knew it. The guards knew it. All the prisoners knew it. It was only a matter of time. Over the last year, I don't know why they hadn't all just got the job over and done with. I then went back to different snippets of conversations I had heard. It was now a year later and my Cantonese was a lot better than the few phrases I spoke when I came in.

I tried to remember the words that I heard, to piece together the tones, the syllables. There was something going on. This was clear; it wasn't me losing it again. That is why I was standing there outside the governor's office waiting to hear my fate. His office was full of high-level guards discussing what the outcome of my life would be. I reached a place of calmness. The same Cantonese words kept coming into my head. The small groups, sometimes just pairs of prisoners having quick whispers to each other whilst looking at me.

'Gat Gwai'.
'Giordano'.
'Hak say woi'.
'Gwai Gi mo gong yeah'.
'Dai lo gong mo da lai, lai ming bat'.

The words I understood but didn't really understand the context. Then there was that time when the si lo said to me about outside friends, inside no friends. I was confused about why I hadn't been seriously got yet. Why had it only been little bits and pieces? Every fight I had been in was because of a single incident. They hadn't just one day set someone on me.

My thoughts were broken when I was called into the room. The governor shouted his findings to me that I couldn't understand and I was ordered out of the door again. I was marched back to my cell and ordered to pick up my meagre possessions. We marched outside and I was taken towards the cat A building. My heart started to race. No way could they be taking me in there ... the house of horrors where the worst of the worst were kept.

But, yes, we went straight to the big double gates. They opened and I was taken inside. We walked across the open courtyard and came to the main doorway. The guard rang the gate bell and there was a lot of clanking from a multitude of locks and the door swung open.

My heart was quite literally in my throat. I had all these preconceived ideas of what behind this gate looked like ... terrifying inmates, a dungeon full of wailing, rows of cells with cannibals licking their lips at me, blood smeared across the walls, more screaming and wailing.

But it was not like any of that.

It was white, almost medical. It was so clean. The cleanest cell block I had ever been in. I was signed in and led towards my cell. At every corner, I was looking for the execution chamber. The one everyone talked about where they used to hang prisoners and where everyone thought they would start hanging again after 1997.

We first went passed the TV room and, sure enough, I caught a glimpse of what could have been it, but I wasn't sure. I was led up some stairs and out onto a landing. We walked past several cells and stood in front of one where the guard opened the barred door.

I was ushered into what was the nicest cell I had been in yet. Brightly lit and immaculately clean. The view was directly at the series of massive razor-wire topped fences and beyond them, the main wall. It seemed that the longer the sentence, the cleaner the cell.

If you were having to spend tens of years in one room with the minimum to entertain you, other than doing thousands of push-ups and sit-ups every day, you cleaned your cell. You cleaned every single part of the cell.

In each cell, there was a small metal plate on the wall, in the middle of which was the call button. This button was to be used only in an emergency and was supposed to bring the guards running. However, I had previously found out that the bell was pressed so often that the guards just ignored it unless it was accompanied by lots of loud shouting.

Loud shouting was one thing I couldn't do that time when I was having an asthma attack but fortunately, an officer walks past the cells every thirty minutes so I didn't have to wait that long.

Anyway, that piece of metal plating could be polished and acted as the only mirror that prisoners ever got the chance of using. The taps could be polished with a bit of toothpaste, it was even possible to make the ancient sink shine as well. This was home and was one of the only things that each prisoner could take pride in.

Every day, I would make sure that my floor was nice and clean as a dusty floor was more likely to attract insects and cockroaches and rats love cockroaches. So, if inmates didn't want the rats nibbling their toes, it was better not to give them a food source. This cell had obviously been loved. Everything was as if it had been done up as a show cell.

'As you can see, Sir, it comes with all amenities and has been lovingly decorated and looked after by its former occupants who were a serial killer and child rapist'.

The light was the brightest that I had ever seen and there was one just as bright outside. It was great; it really gave me a big input of energy, as if I was standing in the sun. If I closed my eyes, I could even imagine I was getting a nice tan on the beach somewhere.

But it was a solitary cell. I hadn't been given any of my books or personal items. I didn't know what was happening really. I thought that I was just being moved into this unit to allow me some peace and quiet. 'Oh yeah', I thought, 'Because that's what they'd do for me, right!' But there I was left.

In the evening, my food was brought to me by one of the occupants of the unit. I had seen him before but had never been this close to him. He had killed his whole family, I found out later.

He was off his face on something and had an argument with them, so he decided to get a meat cleaver and chopped them all to pieces. There was also some talk of him cooking them and raping his little sister's body for a few days until the neighbours were alerted to the rather pungent odour coming from their neighbours next door.

I ate my rice and put my plate out onto the landing through the bars. It was collected sometime later. Because of the lighting, I was totally unaware of the time. Staring through so much light to the outside didn't allow you to be fully able to gauge the time. It wasn't until the lights went on at the main prison wall and the watchtowers put their lights on that I knew it was getting late. The radio then came on so I realised that everyone must be in their cells.

I sat there listening. From some distance awa,y I could hear different radios playing different music. Category A prisoners can get a radio if they earn enough money and are good villains. So, this was what I was hearing. I lay back on my bed and listened to the mixture of distant music.

The radio then went off, but the light didn't. This was new. In fact, the light never went off all night. There I lay with the light shining all night long. I had nothing to even try to cover it. I made my bed and tried to do my normal bedtime routine, but it was virtually impossible because my brain said that this was not the sleepy time. 'It is too bright, you fool' my brain said:

'Get off your bed. Why are you brushing your teeth? It's time to be awake, not asleep.'

It was a terrible night. There was, as usual, the low murmuring of prisoners talking to each other down the corridors. No one shared a cell in this block just in case they tried to eat each other, and that's not in reference to anything sexual. And there were some radios that played for hours. I had no idea if they had forgotten to switch off my light, were keeping it on because I was a suicide risk, or this was just normal in this cell block with the most dangerous young men that had been caught in this part of the world.

The next morning, I got up and made my bed when the radio came on and sat there waiting patiently. My breakfast came – a slice of bread, a slice of cheese and cold milk tea. No change there.

Then my plate was removed and that was it until lunch. I sat there for the rest of the day until dinner -- vegetables, potatoes, some sort of hard meat and cold tea. I ate and my plate was removed. I was there for weeks.

The same routine every day. I saw no one, no one saw me apart from a guard and the family eater. After the first few days, I realised that I was stuck here and had to keep my brain active. I planned a whole exercise routine for myself that would last for a couple of hours.

I did a lot of brain exercises where I would remember a book I had read, and I would re-write it in my head and even play some of the parts and characters. However, my senses were highly attuned to a very high density, and I started to hear, smell, taste and feel so many things.

I also imagined that I could reach out beyond my bars and travel anywhere I wanted to in my mind. I was changing; I was no longer a lad from Scotland, a lowly heroin addict who got mixed up with the local triad. I became a triad leader. I had committed so many terrible crimes. I was the Medusa triad. No one could look at me or they would immediately go insane and become under my control.

I could cause planes to crash or people to murder others just by merely thinking about it. I would start to shun even the tiny human contact I was having. I would wait for them, standing in my cell, but with my back to them. I wouldn't turn when they arrived; I would totally ignore them. It was my only way of having power over my environment.

I was slowly going mad. They say some people can live a long time in isolation, in solitary, and come out quite sane. I wouldn't have been one of those people. I had no idea how long it would take me to go mad as I had lost all knowledge of time, day or night, weekday or weekend. I had even forgotten what month it was. At times, I had no idea where I was or who I was. My dreams had somewhat taken over my reality.

Chapter 29

Summertime was nearly here, my parents were gone, Uncle Malcolm was about to leave and I had a pile of money in my pocket. It was going to be glorious.

Two years ago, I was losing my virginity to a Venezuelan prostitute during two months on the World Texas oil tanker. Last summer I was in the Royal Navy running around with guns over obstacle courses. And now I was here, new city, new me, new attitude. Okay, so I had lost my job recently but there were many more, I'd find one easily during the summer. I just had to pick up the South China Morning Post on a Saturday, close my eyes and point to the job section.

I now had more friends than the number of people I had met over the last sixteen years. Different groups of friends in different places. I had my best friend Melanie and the group we hung around with. Then there were the Thingummy's crowd and the In Place beer buffet gang. If I went to Wan Chai I knew people, Lan Kwai Fong the same. There wasn't anywhere in Hong Kong that I didn't know anyone apart from the dark creepy places like Mong Kok, Tuen Mun and the walled city. You just didn't go to these places as they were filled with triad gangs. You'd read stories of how they would chop you up if you bumped into them.

Yes, I had tried drugs, but I was more interested in the bar scene, hanging out with friends in dark pubs, not hiding out in dark parks and alleyways. I had it all, I didn't need any of that.

第30章

One day without any forewarning, I was unlocked from the torment and taken to the governor's office. On the walk there, I found myself growling. I was acting like an animal in a zoo, albeit a tame one.

I stood outside the governor's office for about an hour before being taken in. There he sat behind his desk with some other officers standing next to him. He spoke to me in English, although I didn't recognise it at first. It had been so long since I had heard it. I just thought it was Chinese. Finally, I realised what he was saying. I was being transferred.

They had no other option as they were unable to put me back into the general population; it would have meant that my life was in danger. They had concrete evidence that I would be killed so they had no other option. I was being transferred tomorrow.

I was dismissed and returned to my solitary cell in A block. To my delight and amazement, all my belongings had been returned to my cell. My books, magazines, papers, letters, toothpaste, towel, and everything. I looked at it all as I was locked in and wept. I realised now that I was going to survive.

I had survived.

I had been fighting for my life for a whole year in the prison. I was mentally damaged to who knows what extent. I was losing the power to talk, constantly lost in my own mind. Not knowing reality from fiction.

The fiction that I was making up in my own mind was extreme paranoia and I was thinking that paranoia was an extreme method of survival. If you are totally paranoid, maybe it helps you to keep away from all possible danger. I didn't think I was being poisoned or that there was a conspiracy, I just couldn't trust anyone, couldn't have my back to anyone.

I used to hear them at night taunting me, telling me what they would do to me, kill me and cut me up into little pieces. It wasn't death that I was frightened of. I didn't want the pain, and it would have been painful. But more than that, I didn't want to lose. I had lost my whole life. Everything that I had tried, I had lost. But now I wanted to win.

I was in the greatest challenge of my life and this time nobody who knew me was watching. Nobody knew what was happening. Before, when my parents didn't turn up to events, it was their choice, but now it wasn't. What was the point of winning anything when your parents quite openly said they had no interest in watching you? They were quite happy that I was out of the house so that they could drink.

My mum quite openly said once that she would never stand at the side of the sports pitch watching me in the cold. Thanks, mum, each time you muttered these things, you stole that competitive edge from me. I never finished anything because what was the point, nobody would cheer.

They never saw me play table tennis or rugby, two sports that I was in school teams for and other local teams as well. If I'd had a little more support, I could have made it into the national table tennis side. They never even got me a good bat to play with. Oh, how I dreamed of a butterfly bat.

They only saw me play cricket once because my dad and his pissed pals organised that match one day and I was made to play.

I made the highest runs and took three wickets, two in my first over. But nobody cared, no one mentioned it. I just walked off the field alone as if I was a ghost.

I remember working hard through the haze of New Year alcohol to get our school's B team into a cricket final against another school's A team but then throwing the game partly due to my health as I had been drinking for eleven straight days and partly as I didn't want to win because there was no point.

My parents just thought I was scum, the black sheep of the family. The black sheep that they created, they were hiding from themselves. They weren't strong enough to admit their own fault in producing me, maybe that's why they drank so much to hide their pain.

But everything is hierarchical. I was not the worst boy in there, that was for sure. I had never murdered or raped, had never physically harmed another human being for fun or for a crime.

I know that I'd hurt people psychologically and for that I am remorseful. I'd had fights in school; I'd had fights out of school. I didn't seek a life of crime. I became a heroin addict and committed crimes to feed my addiction, my mental disease. I can't say I'm blameless, but my parents blamed me.

They said that either I was born bad or that something had made me bad. They never admitted any responsibility as to who I was. They couldn't leave the country quick enough when I was arrested. Never paid for any lawyer to help me. Just left me in a Chinese prison to await my fate. Dumped like a piece of garbage.

No, I wasn't going to lose this battle. I was going to survive.

I had survived, so far.

I was given a chance; this move to another prison. I would go to that prison as a survivor. I knew how my attitude in Pik Uk had caused me so many problems. In my new prison, Lai Sun, I would go in and just be myself. People liked me. I would be careful, but I wouldn't be an arsehole anymore.

I started to pack up my things. I really should have thrown some stuff out but it's difficult to part with things when they are all you have got.

Later that day, a bag was brought to my cell for me to put my things in. It was a large orange jiffy bag just like I had when I was in the Navy. I packed it full. It weighed a ton with all my books. That night, I lay there on my bed thinking of the days to come and the days that had passed. The confusion had gone. The tricks my mind had been playing on me were now distant.

I was no longer lost in a world of despair and mental distress. The last year had been the biggest challenge of my life and I had survived it. Each day had been full of anxiety, threats and the unknown. Every night had been full of nightmares, the yells from the other prisoners of what they would do to me if they could have got their hands on me.

Depression was always there in my cockroach-infested cell. I looked forward to its relative physical safety at night but as soon as I was there, I felt trapped in my own mind. My own thoughts were the enemy, the enemy that could hurt me, attack me. The night-time routines of washing, exercising, and making my bed, the only things that could be seen as normal, as routine.

Thoughts of my own worth would be another constant, the knowledge that I was unloved, uncared for. My family was disgusted by what I had become. How would life be with them on release? Was it worth being released at all? Should I just go out in a thunderclap of violence and excitement? Should I, could I just kill myself here in this concrete shit hole?

But that would have meant giving up, allowing myself to be defeated. I had been defeated all my life up to this point. There was never any reason why I should be victorious. My family let me know that from an early age. Never attending anything I was involved in.

But not now; now I had won. I had won the most challenging part of my life so far. I had survived the constant threats to my life. Okay, so they managed to put me in hospital for a while but I came back. Although I was in a mentally depressed and challenged state, I still managed to survive.

I survived with my back against the wall, with hundreds coming at me. Nobody had managed to slip a sharpened chopstick through my ribs and into my heart. They had not managed to slice me with a piece of metal melted into a toothbrush. I had even managed to fight off four of them with socks filled with soap. I don't know how, but I had. And now I was to go somewhere new.

Chapter 30

I thought nothing more of it, then a month later my dad went off to Korea to work and my mum and brother went to the UK for six weeks for a holiday. They left me in the flat with a pile of cash to keep me going. The only thought I had was beer and party. After the first night of partying, the only thought I had from then on was heroin.

Everyone was invited. Just had to see mum and my brother off at the airport, rush back to 7-Eleven grab as much beer and ice as I could, catch a cab and get back home. Then I needed to chuck all the beer and ice into the bath, clear all the furniture out of the front room, get my brother's ghetto blaster, and get the tunes pumping. I didn't have to wait long. By 8.00 pm, the flat was full and everyone was pissed.

I knew most of the people there but not all. A few old girlfriends had shown up, but everyone was being cool. I wasn't snogging anyone at that time. People were dancing, others playing drinking games. The three bedrooms were getting used for sex, a proper teenage party. Mick turned up with a posse. He introduced me to them one by one. The last one said, 'Hi, I'm Sam.'

She was tall, blonde, slim, and hot. Although there were plenty of hot girls there, she had something about her, I was transfixed with her and it appeared that the feeling was mutual. We stood there staring at each other for what felt like too long. I shook myself out of it and showed them the bar.

For the next hour or so I would turn round and there she was, staring at me. However, I was being the host-with-the-most, making sure everyone was happy, chatting to everyone and making sure that they were all having a good time.

There were going to be six weeks of parties, I had to make sure everyone was happy. So, for the most part, I ignored her. Quite late into the night, I got a tap on my shoulder, I turned and there she was.

'Can you get me another drink?' she asked.

'Sure,' I said, and went off to the bathroom. I leant over the bath and grabbed two cans, one for her and one for me. When I stood up and turned round to head back to her in the living room, I found her standing right behind me. She had followed me into the bathroom; she had locked the door, and then she pinned me up against the wall, stuck her face against mine, stuck her tongue in my mouth and pushed her whole body against me. She was hot, even feverish, sucking my face, grinding her body against mine, groaning and panting, whispering some quite vulgar but extremely hot things into my ears.

She had her hands down my trousers in a flash and had undone the buttons of my 501s. She then dropped to her knees and inhaled my cock deep into her hot mouth. I stood there, not knowing what to do with the two cans of lager that I was holding as they were wet and dripping. I didn't want them to drip onto her and put her off her stride, so I managed to nearly dislocate my shoulder and put them on the bathroom window shelf. I thought I had put her off because she got up, but she pushed me back against the wall, and whilst staring intensely at me she pulled, one at a time, the straps of her dress of her shoulders allowing her dress to fall to the ground. She had no bra on and her gorgeous tits seemed to be asking me to touch them.

But before I could, whilst still staring at me she almost unperceptively pulled her panties down to reveal a beautifully manicured pussy. She then stepped towards me, grabbed me and pushed me down onto the toilet, turned around and with her pert little ass pointed at me grabbed my cock and lowered herself down on to me, guiding me straight and deep into her.

She leant back on me and started riding me with the most amazing desire that I had ever witnessed. I reached around and found her amazingly hard tits and her nipples. She gasped as I touched them and I could feel her whole body react to the pleasure. She grabbed my right hand away from her tit and placed it hard against her pussy and, using her hand, she rubbed my hand hard and fast against her. She started to groan louder and louder, her body started to shake and said:

'I'm going to come, I'm going to come, please come with me now, please come with me now!'

And with that, we both reached our peak at the same time. She was thrashing about with each wave of orgasm, and whilst still sitting there she grabbed my cock out of her and started massaging me, up and down. I was still coming and it felt amazing.

She climbed down to the floor and slowly and carefully took my cock into her mouth again. She used her tongue and her mouth to expertly get me going again and within a few minutes, I was coming again this time deep into her mouth. She looked up at me, with hair sticking to her face, and smiled. She then whispered, 'Would you like to do some number 4 with me?'

I think she could have asked me to do just about anything right then and I would have said yes. She got up, pulled her panties back on, picked her dress up off the floor and lifted it above her head so her body was at full stretch and her beautiful tits filled my world for another moment. Then they were gone beneath the loose summer dress that she was wearing. I sorted myself out whilst watching her, she then slipped her hand into her dress where there was a little pocket for unneeded, for her anyway, padding and pulled out a little bundle tied together by some fine string. She unwrapped it by the sink.

Wrapped in cloth were a little silver tube and a small silver box. She opened the box to reveal the magic white powder inside. With her fingernail she took some of the powder out, closed the box and tipped the powder onto the lid. She took the little tube and quickly sniffed the powder up her nose. She pinched her nose, threw her head back, held it for a while and then brought her head back forward and let out a little sigh.

She opened the box again and used her nail to take out a little more and put it onto the box lid for me. I took the tube and sniffed at the powder. But unfortunately, I didn't plan my breath properly so, instead of sniffing the powder up my nose, I ended up blowing most of it off the box.

'Watch what you're doing, for fuck's sake', she screamed.

She took the tube from me.

'I'll show you how to do it', she said.

She snorted the remaining powder herself and took some more out for me.

'Now take the tube and place it next to one nostril and with your other finger, close your other nostril', she instructed.

'Blow the air out of your lungs, away from the smack then bend down and inhale.'

I followed her word for word and expertly took my line. As soon as I did, I started to gag again but she did an amazing thing, she grabbed my face and started kissing me hard. It had to be one of the sexiest kisses I had ever had. The ecstasy of that kiss and the sex before mixed up with the power of that white drug was so intoxicating.

We floated out of the bathroom and back to the party. I felt wonderful, like the king of the party scene, the king of the world and everything around me. We spent the rest of the night stuck to each other drinking, talking and taking more smack. By 5.00 am, there were only a handful of people left. Some were unconscious, others totally out of their faces on drink and smack. Some were smoking joints.

We had run out of drink and the smack was nearly all gone. Those who were still awake decided to head off to Wan Chai to see what we could find. We jumped into Mick's car and went hunting for more.

Coming Soon

Number 4

A Chinese Prison Story

Part 2

Lai Sun

Stewart Burton

第一章

I woke in the morning before the radio went off and got myself fully dressed and packed ready for the exciting day ahead. The guards came to my cell early. I backed up to the bars as I had done many times before so that the two guards could handcuff me, one holding my arms, one putting the cuffs on, and another watching over the whole process for safety reasons.

Once they were satisfied, I was told to move to the rear of the cell so that the other guard could open it safely. I was then called forward to exit the cell and told to turn around so that one guard could take one of my arms on each side. One guard handcuffed me before letting me out of the cell, because of my high level of security even though it had been lowered for my transfer.

I was taken out of my cell before anyone else and brought to the dining hall. The only other people there were remanded prisoners on their way to court. After breakfast, we were taken to the reception where I sat and waited. The others were given their court clothes to change into.

Immediately I could see the ones who were loved and the ones with no one. The loved ones had new clothes to put on, the designer brands: Giordano, Benetton, the shell suits and the new trainers. The unloved and uncared for had only the clothes in which they had been arrested, a totally unfair system. We judge someone within the first few seconds of meeting them, so the ones with the new clothes had an advantage over the ones who looked and smelt terrible.

And if the unloved had been unfortunate enough to have been arrested during the summer, whilst wearing their t-shirts, shorts and flip-flops, they were going to freeze now during the winter as that was all they had to wear, all day.

I looked at them all and pondered who they were and where they were going. At least I was partly through my sentence. I had hope, I knew when I was going to be released, and they were right at the beginning. They would still be given opportunities to shorten their sentence, to become a grass and get a reduced tariff. But everyone knew what happened to grasses, they had no chance. When released -- if they survived their sentence -- somebody would be waiting for them outside.

Take the sentence. What were they going to get: 5 years, 10, 15, 20? Who knew? They could get let off. They could be found not guilty ... that was always the dream, for the system to fail and let you go by mistake. The prison is full of innocent prisoners; convictions depend on how the court was feeling. It also depended on the lawyers. I didn't have a paid lawyer, I didn't deserve one paid for by my parents. They got out of the country as quickly as they could to hide themselves from their disappointment as to how their son had turned out.

Of course, I should have turned out just fine. Who needs their parents to bring them up, support them, love them? My parents used alcohol every day to release them from this burden and how dare I use substances as well to unburden myself. They left me to my own problems, so they got what they deserved. I then thought of my own release again. What would be the point of going back to them? They didn't like me or want me. They never wanted me to win, to be the best.

But now, as I was getting my ankles and wrists shackled to my waist and taken to the high-security van, I knew I had won. I had beaten the system that had tried to beat me. I was alive and kicking and ready for my next adventure.

That was it. I was going on an adventure. I wasn't going to anything as bad as what I had just gone through. I was on the up. I was going somewhere better and for the first time in my life, I had won!

Stewart Burton

Thirty years is a long time ago. The dreams still keep me awake; old injuries from back then now begin to hurt more.

I am Scottish, autistic and this is my story of spending three years in a Chinese prison.

Those years cured me of my addiction to heroin and saved my probable death from either addiction, an armed robbery gone wrong or the Hong Kong triad, either the gang I was in or another.

In prison, I knew within the first two weeks that I was in danger when I saw someone stabbed to death in front of me. Suicide by hanging was common, fights daily and the brutality of the guards was part of everyday life.

The first half of my sentence was spent in maximum security and the remainder in an ex-leper colony in the South China Sea.

Ashamed, I kept my story to myself for many years. I have tried to repay my debt to society by using my experience to support others.

A founding member of the award-winning Routes Out of Prison project in Scotland, I was the first ex-offender and drug addict to be allowed to work inside some of Scotland's prisons, mainly in HMP Barlinnie and the women's prison HMP Cornton Vale.

Six months of gaining the guards' trust and then I was permitted to go where I needed to. I was also the first ex-offender to go through specialised breakaway training and control and restraint training.

I have since been diagnosed with Asperger's Syndrome. Shortly afterwards, I managed to talk my way onto the MSc Autism course at the University of Strathclyde. Not having a Bachelor's degree I couldn't qualify from the course, but it launched me into the area of neurodiversity. I also attended the University of Glasgow and qualified as a person-centred counsellor during this time.

Believing in early intervention, I decided to apply to become a member of the Scottish Children's Panel. This is unique to Scotland, a court system for children who have either committed an offence or are causing concern or who have had an offence committed against them. Similar to being a magistrate with three panel members for every case.

The application form was incredibly detailed and required many hours of careful consideration to complete it. When it was ready I placed it in the return envelope with my criminal record on the very top of it. Thinking that they would take one look and turn me down. They didn't. They asked me for an interview in front of ten people.

After a few more interviews I was offered a place on the training course and after completing that I became the first ex-offender, ex-addict and openly autistic member of the Children's Panel.

I was made redundant and decided to spend a year travelling in India. That turned into 8 years.

It wasn't until 2017, when I returned to my old school in Hong Kong that I started the journey of writing these two books.

Martin Lever

International award-winning Artist Martin Lever lived, studied and worked in Hong Kong on and off for nearly 40 years before his recent relocation to North Yorkshire. One of the biggest inspirations in his life is the unique Asian city he was lucky to call home. And he's now embracing a new muse - the dramatic environment surrounding his new home in Marrick in the Yorkshire Dales National Park.

His contemporary artwork has been exhibited in a number of solo shows in Hong Kong, the UK and the Middle East. His work adorns the walls of private collectors, and commissioned pieces hang in corporate lobbies from Estee Lauder to Wharf Group, from the McKinsey corporation to Patton Boggs Law.

His approach to painting is refreshingly simple: he closes his eyes, then paints what he sees. Using striking contrasts of colour and lighthearted observational touches, he creates powerful abstract and pop-art expressionist images that celebrate the world around us through a new
lens.

Beyond art, his creative work has been recognised around the world with countless advertising industry awards. And his acclaimed series of children's books – The BogeyBugz – is helping fuel young imaginations.

Awards
Grand Prix, Golds, Silvers and Bronzes at a range of local, regional and international creativity
festivals and shows...including
Cannes Festival of Creativity, New York Festivals, London International Awards, D&AD Awards, HK Kam Fan – Best in Show 2017

Matt Ellis

Matt Ellis is an Independent Singer/Songwriter based in California. Born in Australia and raised in Hong Kong, Matt attended Island School at the same time as Stewart, studying in the grade below. Matt's path to music began at the school, forming the band "The Underground" with fellow students, playing at school dances, fetes, and local bars. Stewart's book resonated with Matt greatly, having first-hand experience with the school, city, timeline, lead, and supporting characters.

The story haunted him, taking him back to that incredible time when teenagers were exploring new freedoms and discovering hidden layers of a city that no longer exists. Matt was so taken by "Number 4" that he was inspired to write a song based on the book, written from Stewart's p.o.v. and experience. The song, "Number 4", will be released this year and feature prominently on Stewart's Podcast.

With a sound on the Rock end of the Americana genre, Matt's music has taken him across Australia, The United States, Canada, Hong Kong, and Mexico sharing the stages with Calexico, Paul Kelly, DeVotchKa, Kasey Chambers, LeAnn Rimes and John Doe to name a few. Album guests have included Nels Cline, Greg Leisz, and Merry Clayton and numerous tracks have been licensed by Sony PlayStation, Audible, ABC, LMN, MTV, Qantas, and The Food Network while receiving airplay on dozens of Radio Stations around the globe.

Matt is now focussed on his 7th Album, working with Nicolas Vernhes (War On Drugs, Spoon, Silver Jews), and plans to release more new material this year. Visit www.mattellis.com for more info.

Zara Morris

Zara was born in Hong Kong and went to Island School from 1980 to 1985, leaving for sixth form and university in England, four years before Stewart arrived.

She returned straight after university to complete her legal training. She qualified as a solicitor and practised there for many years before leaving in 2012. Having spent some time in Hong Kong's criminal courts, Zara has had firsthand experience of Hong Kong's criminal justice system. The city, as it was, will always hold a very special place in her heart.

Hong Kong was generally safe so some parents allowed their kids to roam freely as long as they were home in time for their curfew, which Stewart was not given. Any of them could have ended up down the same route.